I0815465

WILD DYEING

FROM THE GARDEN TO COLOR

AN INTRODUCTION TO NATURAL VEGETABLE DYES

TEXT AND PHOTOGRAPHS
Céline Philippe

New York · Paris · London · Milan

CONTENTS

INTRODUCTION

My passion for plants has led me down the path of botanical color, a perpetual display of nature's intelligence, inventiveness, richness, and virtues. I started out with an interest in the aromatic and medicinal properties of plants, especially those formerly known as "simples," which were traditionally cultivated in one's garden for nourishment and medicine. Then I discovered that, quite often, the same plants that are good for eating and treating ailments could also produce color. We should feel humbled in the face of such ingenuity.

After becoming invested in what I was putting on my plate and how I was caring for my body, it was only logical for me to start caring about what I wore, especially concerning the colors of our textiles.

It is well-known that the textile industry is one of the most polluting in the world, second only to agribusiness. This is particularly true for the dyeing sector.

In this regard, an increasing number of textile creators are adopting an eco-friendly approach that shows the traceability of their products as well as their impact on the environment and our health. In this emerging slow-fashion movement, supply chains for more ethical textiles are gradually being developed, with special attention being paid to the nature and origin of the textile fiber, its manufacturing process, and its carbon footprint.

The industrial dyeing sector is currently undergoing significant development. In France and elsewhere, start-ups are researching environmentally friendly dyeing processes using non-petroleum-based colorants, which is the case of all industrially manufactured dyes. The rise of green chemistry will certainly allow fashion industry professionals in the future to assert that their colors are natural and eco-friendly. This will be a real "revolution" because until now, natural dyeing has only existed through artisanal production methods.

Will this announced "revolution" mean the death of artisanal vegetal dyeing? I don't think so. Producing a color on a large scale that is identical every time is not the same process as making your own colors with plants that you yourself have harvested or chosen. The satisfaction derived from the labor of your own hands and the meaning given to it by working with natural materials fulfill an essential need for many of us. Skills like growing your own vegetables and making your own clothes, household products, and cosmetics are becoming increasingly necessary in our time so that we can relearn what has been forgotten, create a connection with the living world around us, and better preserve it. Therefore, I propose (re)discovering this ancestral knowledge that has colored centuries past.

Throughout history, humans have made color using the resources around them, especially plants.

My passion for plants thus led me to delve into the processes of plant dyeing, as people have practiced for centuries. Dominique Cardon, a researcher at the French National

Centre for Scientific Research (CNRS), has explored the wonderful world of natural dyes across cultures and history.

Early on for me, mordanting seemed like a crucial aspect for those wishing to create ecological and sustainable dyes. It is the first step in the dyeing process, a decisive step that creates an affinity between the fiber to be dyed and the plant dye: the mordant establishes a strong bond between the plant dye and the fiber to ensure the color holds. In other words, mordanting enables the color to last over time. The mordant is, in a way, the fixative.

Metal ions primarily work as the fixing agents. That is why dyers in the past traditionally used aluminum, copper, iron, as well as chrome, tin, and lead sulfates to fix their colors. Today, the use of heavy metals such as tin, lead, and chromium as mordants has been abandoned due to their adverse health effects.

But what about aluminum, known as alum, which many use today for mordanting plant dyes? As a mordant, alum comes in the form of salts: alum salts or aluminum salts, a white powder of either natural or synthetic origin. Regardless of their manufacturing method, these aluminum salts come from bauxite mines whose exploitation, especially in countries in the Southern Hemisphere, is disastrous for the environment and local populations. Furthermore, the safety of aluminum in the form of salts for our health is debated.

I quickly abandoned the use of alum salts as a mordant. Besides their harmful effects on nature and health, all the precautions needed to handle the white powder, such as wearing gloves and a mask, frightened me a little, not to mention the question of where to dispose of the mordant bath safely without risk of pollution.

When I initially started exploring plant-based dyeing, I naively thought that plant-based colors were made solely from plants. Determined to work only with plants to create color, I then explored the existing alternatives to alum.

First, there are all the plants that textiles can be dyed with without the need for a mordant. In dyer's jargon, these are referred to as "substantive colors" as opposed to "adjective colors." Onion, avocado, and turmeric are among the most well-known in this category. There are also all the plants that yield indigo. Indigo, a unique plant in the world of natural dyes, offers a dyeing process without the need for mordanting.

But for other plants and other colors, the mordanting step is indispensable. In the absence of alum salts, certain plants can take on the role of mordant. In fact, in other times and places, dyers did not always have access to alum in their surroundings. Yet this did not prevent them from creating color from local plant resources. They had a rich knowledge of local plants and knew that some had the ability to create this alchemy that unites the natural dye with the natural fiber.

This is true of plants naturally rich in alumina or oxalic acid, as well as tannin-rich plants. I experimented with plants whose use as mordants was traditionally proven. Enthusiastically, I also ventured down other paths with plants that are more readily accessible. Reading, experimenting, and researching were necessary to familiarize myself with these plant mordants. To accurately assess their effectiveness, I first tested emblematic dye plants known for the durability of their colors. Then, I continued my experiments by combining plant-based mordants with local plants, cultivated or wild, that had dyeing properties worthy of interest.

When working with plants, the process of natural dyeing is slower and more demanding.

As in gardening, you must know how to observe in order to understand what is happening. You must intervene wisely, taking time to appreciate this process of revealing plant colors. It is an exhilarating experience that awakens the senses: the smell of the baths, the feel of the natural fibers, and the sight of the color of the dyes slowly rising on the fibers.

I love this creative experience, the revelation of a plant's color. And as nature is inherently generous, the color offered by plants is not the expression of a single dye but of a multitude of dyes. This is what characterizes plant colors: rich, deep hues.

Creating with plant colors is thus a way to connect with nature and its biodiversity. Because you know the hidden colors of plants, you pay special attention to weeds, to the spontaneity of the countryside, to plant waste. These plants become, in your eyes, "useful" plants, plants to preserve and protect, like hidden treasures.

I hope that this book will allow you to look at certain unjustly spurned wild plants in a different light. Undeniably, creating colors solely from plants is an extension of a life philosophy oriented toward living things and respecting biodiversity.

Today, we live in a complex world in the midst of transformation, reaching the limits of a paradigm that is unsustainable because it is destroying our natural environment. It is difficult, under these circumstances, even when we have the will to do otherwise, not to be trapped by certain contradictions. That is why, when I dye, I reconcile with myself. I hope this book will allow you to share this sentiment.

PART 1

A FEW FUNDAMENTALS TO KNOW BEFORE GETTING STARTED

RAW MATERIALS

Fibers for dyeing

When you are interested in plant-based colors, you generally prefer natural materials. In this, the project of plant dyeing is consistent: both the materials and colors are derived from the living world.

All sorts of natural materials can be dyed with plants: wood, willow, paper, skins, and all textile fibers, whether of animal or plant origin. I will share my dyeing experience here with numerous textile fibers, in the form of skeins of yarn or fabric, woven or knitted.

Distinction of fibers according to their origin

1 · Fibers of animal origin: wool and silk

- **Wool** is made from the fleece of animals such as sheep, alpacas, mohair goats, angora rabbits, camels, and even yaks. There is currently a real movement in France and other parts of the world to revitalize the wool industry, which is part of an environmentally friendly approach that aims to perpetuate ancestral know-how. Feel free to explore various local events organized throughout the year around wool and knitting in order to find beautiful wool.

- **Silk** is made from the cocoons of the silkworm caterpillar. Originating from China, this moth has been bred and selected for silk production for millennia. Completely domesticated, *Bombyx mori* can no longer survive without human intervention. It no longer exists in the wild and is unable to feed itself or fly.

Since both of these fibers are made "on the backs" of animals, they should be chosen with care.

For wool, make sure its origin and shearing conditions are respectful of the animal, without the inhumane practice of mulesing.

For silk, opt for "Ahimsa (nonviolent) silk," which spares the lives of the pupa, unlike the ancestral practice of boiling the cocoons with the living insect inside.

2 · Fibers of plant origin: cotton, linen, hemp, and ramie

For plant-derived fibers, the mode of production and cultivation will guide your choices.

- Cultivated in the Global South, **cotton** is water- and treatment-intensive. Organic cotton cultivation is therefore preferable.

- On the other hand, **linen** has the immense advantage of being available locally. France is the world's leading producer of linen. Moreover, its cultivation requires no irrigation and uses few inputs.

- Like linen, **hemp** is not water-intensive and can be grown locally. It has other significant environmental advantages: it grows quickly and requires neither fertilizers nor pesticides. It also plays a major role in soil regeneration since, unlike linen, it has the ability to store CO_2 in the soil.

- **Ramie**, or China grass, grows mainly in countries with tropical climates. It requires warmth and humidity and does not tolerate droughts well. China is the largest producer of ramie and one of the few countries to master its complex production methods.

Whether the fibers come from animals or plants, I advise you to choose those that have undergone as few treatments as possible (such as the superwash treatment for wool or bleaching for cotton, linen, or hemp). And always try to be coherent in your creative approach: work with what nature offers us without spoiling it.

Distinction of fibers in plant-based dyeing

In natural dyeing, it is customary to distinguish between animal fibers and plant fibers because the method of treating them differs.

The protein nature of animal fibers, much like hair and nails, gives them a very good affinity with plant color. It is easy to achieve rich, bright colors. Their preparation for dyeing is relatively simple. However, some precautions are necessary during the dyeing process to avoid damaging the fiber.

- **Wool** is worked at high temperatures. The heat opens the scales of the fiber, allowing it to "grab" the color. Wool can tolerate temperatures up to boiling. However, it dislikes sudden temperature changes from hot to cold, which risks felting. This is a point of vigilance to keep in mind throughout the dyeing process. Always ensure, during any rinsing, that the water temperature is similar to that of the dye bath.

  Similarly, wool does not appreciate high alkaline baths. Here, too, there is a risk of felting with a pH above 9 or even less for some very delicate wools.

  In the interest of preserving the softness of the fiber, I do not iron wool, as it tends to make the fiber rough.

- **Silk**, on the other hand, is generally worked at cold or lukewarm temperatures to avoid damaging its luster.

Such precautions are not necessary for plant fibers. They are all-terrain fibers: they tolerate variations in temperature, significant pH differences, and are not affected by ironing. In this regard, plant fibers are easier to handle.

However, as a trade-off, their cellulose nature sometimes makes it difficult for the dye to adhere to them. The preparation and mordanting steps are therefore long and complex. Plant fibers require more preparation steps for the color to adhere to the fiber in a lasting manner. The resulting shades are also more matte and paler than those achievable with wool and silk.

Finally, no matter what kind of fiber you use, its quality and how it was manufactured will influence the color outcome.

Dyeing old household linens is often the first idea that comes to mind when venturing into plant color. These fabrics, which have already lived a long life, can offer us pleasant surprises. However, they retain the marks of their past use: plant dyeing will not make stains disappear; on the contrary, it can even reveal them.

What to do if you do not know whether a fabric or thread is natural or synthetic, animal or plant

How do you find out? The flame test will tell you. Gently bring the fiber close to the flame and observe:

- if it burns slowly, with a smell of burnt hair, goes out by itself, leaving behind a small pile of charred beads as ash, it is an animal fiber (wool or silk).
- if it burns quickly, without any particular smell, leaving little ash, it is a plant fiber (linen, cotton, hemp, etc.).
- if it burns quickly, leaving behind a hard black ball like burnt plastic, it is a synthetic fiber.

	Pros	Cons
Plant fibers	Resistant to: • changes in temperature • high pH bases • ironing	• Colors are less vivid and more matte • Lengthy preparation and mordanting
Animal fibers	• Faster preparation and mordanting • Bright, rich colors	Handling precautions: • must avoid sudden temperature changes • do not tolerate high pH levels or bases

Plants

In my completely plant-based dyeing practice, I usually distinguish between mordant plants and dye plants.

The former are useful for the mordanting stage, while the latter are used for the dye bath.

That being said, the distinction is somewhat artificial. Most plants have more than one resource within them. And certain plants, due to their particular chemical composition, can be used for both coloring and "fixing" the color.

The merit of this distinction is merely to clarify ideas for a more methodological approach.

Mordant plants

As explained in the introduction, it is primarily metal ions that work as a mordant to bind an organic dye to a natural fiber. The most universal and widely used in the world of natural dyes is aluminum, the most abundant metal in the Earth's crust. One of the reasons for its success is that it does not affect colors, unlike iron or copper.

Since the Middle Ages, alum, derived from aluminum, has been manufactured and used as a mordant. The manufacturing processes have evolved over time, from the traditional and ancient alum stone to the more recent aluminum sulfate, whose uses today are diverse.

However, not all people around the world had access to alum, due to either geographical or economic reasons. Nevertheless, this did not prevent them from creating color with local plants.

1 • Aluminum-accumulator plants

Plants absorb a number of micronutrients through their roots that they need for their metabolism. Along with water, metal ions in the soil can be absorbed by the root system and transported through the sap to the plant's storage organs, the leaves (or bark for trees).

When a plant is capable of absorbing and storing significant amounts of metal ions (Al for aluminum), it is called an "accumulator plant" or "hyperaccumulator plant."

Several conditions, including climate and soil factors, influence the plant's ability to accumulate Al or any other metal ion. In particular, the lower the soil's pH, the more aluminum is available in the soil and able to be absorbed by hyperaccumulator plants.

Thanks to the incredible abilities of these plants, artisanal dyers—in other times or today in different latitudes—turn to this plant "alum," which replaces mineral alum.

These two mordants, one of mineral origin and the other plant-based, have in common the Al ion to designate aluminum, but the comparison stops there. Their molecular structures are quite different; a difference that is also found in the shades of colors that result from the dyeing process, which will not be identical depending on whether you use mineral or plant "alum."

The majority of identified aluminum hyperaccumulator plants originate in tropical and subtropical climates. The most well-known and widespread are those belonging to the genus *Symplocos*: trees and shrubs found in tropical to temperate regions in Asia, India, and Japan.

Other shrubs of the Melastomataceae family, native to the Pacific and Central America, have been valued in dyeing with the same properties.

In Europe, lycopods, a class of herbaceous perennial plants resembling mossy ferns, have been used as plant mordants in Scotland and Germany. Found in peat bogs and wetlands, this species is endangered. Harvesting it for use as a plant mordant would therefore be the opposite of an environmentally friendly approach.

For me, it seems more consistent and responsible in this case to prefer symplocos. Like some spices in our meals, or like chocolate and tea that are difficult to do without, symplocos comes from afar, certainly, but its carbon impact is reduced as long as its harvesting is respectful of the plant and living things. It also supports local artisan economies, and the environmental footprint of its supply is rather positive. More local and accessible plants such as hydrangeas and camellias (see photo p. 14) are capable to a lesser extent of accumulating aluminum available in the soil in their leaves, provided that the soil is acidic and rich in aluminum. The blue color of hydrangeas is a good indicator of this accumulation ability.

Black tea (*Camellia sinensis*) is a naturally aluminum-accumulating plant, making it one of the major sources of aluminum intake in food.

Numerous scientific studies have focused on aluminum concentrations in tea. The results show that the total metal content of tea leaves differs depending on the type of tea. It is influenced by many factors, such as the physical and chemical properties of the soil, as well as the maturation time of the leaves.

However, according to these studies, consuming tea is not considered dangerous. And keeping its leaves after infusion can be interesting for dyeing. I will come back to this later.

2 · Plants rich in iron and other trace elements

Strictly speaking, there are no plants that accumulate iron, but only plants that are naturally rich in iron. Plants only take in the amount of iron they need for their metabolism.

In Latin America, the roots of dock plants are traditionally used as a mordant on wool. Their high iron content certainly justifies this use.

Iron, including that of plant origin, greatly alters the shade of colors produced in dyeing, with a strong tendency to darken them. This should be taken into account when integrating iron into a dyeing process.

Plants naturally rich in iron generally contain a significant amount of tannins, which also play an important role in dyeing.

Other easily accessible plants rich in trace elements, such as nettle and other aromatic plants, could be the subject of research and experiments to contribute to the mordanting of fibers that you want to dye.

I have been able to experiment with some of them. I will discuss this in the section on the dyeing process.

3 · Tannin plants

Tannins are ubiquitous in the plant world. There is a great diversity of tannins, which differ widely in their size and chemical structure. Located in the vacuoles and cell walls of plants, they can represent 15 to 25 percent of the weight of leaves, and up to 40 percent of the weight of bark, or even 50 percent in some gallnuts.

These chemical compounds of the polyphenol family are used by plants (trees, flowering plants, etc.) as a means of chemical defense against pathogens and herbivores. Their strong astringency quickly deters any animals wanting to graze on them.

Wood, barks, and tree galls generally have the highest concentrations of tannic molecules in trees such as oak, chestnut, acacia, alder, pistachio, fustic, and sumac.

Some fruits are equally interesting, such as tara pods or pomegranate peels.

Tannins have been known since ancient times. In the Middle Ages, they were mainly used for leather preparation: they were extracted from oak or chestnut barks and ground in specific mills in order to obtain a powder that was marketed under the name "tan," hence the term "tannin." The skins were then soaked in tanning pits for at least a year before being processed. Since tannins easily bind to animal skin through strong and irreversible bonds, the skin becomes imperishable once tanned, becoming rotproof, more resistant, and flexible.

From a biological point of view, tannins are classified into two categories, an interesting distinction to know in plant-based dyeing. First, there are the so-called hydrolyzable tannins, which include gallotannins and ellagitannins. In plant-based dyeing, these tannins are mainly used to prepare plant fibers. Their molecular structure enables them to create hooks so that the color binds better to the fiber. Another advantage of hydrolyzable tannins

is that they are generally not very colorfast, so they have little influence on the color obtained.

Then there are condensed tannins. These have the same properties as hydrolyzable tannins when it comes to preparing fibers for dyeing. Since they have a more complex chemical composition, they are also known as proanthocyanidins. Linked to a chemical compound in the flavonoid family, they can be a source of color. For example, this is the particularity of catechu: highly concentrated in condensed tannin, it was once used to dye ships' sails red. This dye acted as a kind of tanning, protecting the fabric from mildew.

The specific chemical properties of tannins are therefore invaluable not only in helping natural dyes bind to plant fibers but also in making color. That is why, to make things simpler, I'll call them color tannins from now on.

What's more, all tannins have the ability to react in the presence of iron to produce blacks and grays. Gallnuts and iron salts are the basic ingredients in the manufacture of black inks. This chemical reaction between plant tannins and iron is very useful for identifying tannin-rich plants around your home (see table at right).

Finally, it appears that when combined with the dyeing process, tannins significantly improve the ultraviolet (UV) resistance of plant colors.

In short, tannins are virtually indispensable in plant-based dyeing.

Following the steps in the table,you can create a lasting herbarium of tannin plants. Once you have washed your fabric, you will have very strong tannin plant prints.

4 · Plants rich in oxalic acid

Industrially produced oxalic acid is traditionally used to dye wool. This acid has a particular affinity with proteins.

Oxalic acid, also known as oxalate, is an organic acid found in many plants. It was therefore natural for me to be interested in plants rich in oxalic acid for use as a mordant on animal fibers.

Rhubarb leaves are well-known for their high oxalic acid content. The same is true of dock,

IDENTIFYING TANNIN PLANTS

1	Harvest leaves from trees, aromatic plants, and wild herbaceous plants.
2	While still fresh, place them flat one by one on a square of undyed cotton or linen cloth, with the upper side of the leaf on top and the most veined side against the fabric.
3	Secure each leaf to the fabric with adhesive tape, such as painter's tape or masking tape.
4	Turn the fabric over onto a flat, smooth, solid surface, such as a cutting board.
5	Using a rubber mallet, carefully tap each leaf until you see its imprint.
6	Turn the fabric over and remove the adhesive.
7	Gently remove plant debris.
8	Fill a container that can allow the fabric to lie flat with water and add 2 cups of iron water (see recipe p. 58) or a spoonful of iron sulfate previously dissolved in a little hot water. Mix well.
9	Plunge the fabric into the container so that it is lying flat at the bottom. The green prints will turn black. This is the visible proof of the presence of tannins.

knotweed, and beet leaves. All these plants can be used as mordants to dye wool and silk.

This brief overview of mordant plants is by no means exhaustive. There's still so much to learn and discover about natural mordants and plant mordants!

Such a classification of plants according to their properties should not obscure the fact that a plant rarely possesses just one active ingredient. Some plants combine several assets, making them multipurpose. They can then be usefully incorporated into dye recipes as both mordants and color plants.

Dye plants

Many plants contain dyes. Their concentration varies considerably depending on species, soil, and climate.

Unlike a synthetic color, plant color is rich in nuances. A single plant can contain between ten and twenty coloring molecules, while a synthetic dye has only seven.

This diversity of plant colorants makes it possible to play with the different nuances. It provides a palette of colors that can be considerably broadened, depending on the dyeing process used. This discovery of a thousand and one plant-based colors is fascinating and guides me in my practice. What is important to me is not so much making a particular color, but exploring the palette of colors a plant can offer.

From a biochemical point of view, plant colorants are organic molecules classified into different families. These families generally correspond to groups of colors.

1 • Flavonoids: yellow plants and so much more . . .

Flavonoids are very present in the plant world and play an essential role for plants: they color the petals to attract foraging insects. They also help plants combat all kinds of stress, notably by protecting them from the sun's rays.

For some years now, medical research has been taking an interest in flavonoids. Numerous studies have demonstrated their health benefits, thanks to their antifungal, antiviral, and antioxidant properties. Flavonoids also play a role in preventing cardiovascular risks and certain cancers. In fact, all medicinal plants contain flavonoids.

The vast majority of flavonoids are yellow. To use Dominique Cardon's expression, it is as if "yellow, the color of the sun that makes plants grow, remained there . . . as if imprisoned."

Thus, many flavonoid-rich plants produce yellows that vary in intensity and stability.

Among the plants that contain a high concentration of flavonoids, making them suitable for vegetable dyeing, we find dyer's rocket, Canadian goldenrod, dyer's chamomile and other chamomiles, yarrow, tansy, dahlia flowers, ragwort, broom flowers, artichoke leaves, sage, and certainly many more.

The dyes in these plants—such as luteolin, rutin, quercetin, and kaempferol—produce rather stable yellows.

Because of their particular structure, some dyes in the flavonoid family create particularly intense orangey yellows, such as those found in cosmos flowers, tickseed, and the European smoketree.

The flavonoid family is not always synonymous with yellow. Thanks to their particular structure, the palettes of some colorants can broaden to include pinks, reds, violets, and bluish hues.

First, there are the anthocyanins, a group of well-known colorants that, historically, have not been widely used by dyers. And for good reason: they are pH sensitive. In fact, they are well-known as pH indicators: they appear red, pink, or violet in an acidic environment, but turn blue or even bluish-gray in alkaline environments. You may have experienced this without knowing it, with a bright red stain from wine or red fruit on a white tablecloth that turns gray after washing.

Redberries, grapes, blackberries, elderberries, blueberries, privet, and ivy are all rich in anthocyanins. They produce bright colors in shades of red, pink, and violet, which unfortunately are not very strong or stable. However, as the resource is considerable, dyers have developed a host of recipes, with varying degrees of success, to stabilize anthocyanin-based colors.

This is not the case with brazilin and hematoxylin, two sources of color that are virtually indispensable in natural dyeing. Both are found in logwood, sappanwood, and brazilwood trees.

Like anthocyanins, they are very rich in dyes and can offer beautiful shades of violet, red, and pink. But brazilin and hematoxylin have the advantage of being much stronger and more stable than anthocyanins.

These plants have long been imported for dyeing purposes. In Europe, they have left their mark on the colors of centuries past. The black suits of the nineteenth century, for example, were all made from logwood.

What all these flavonoid dyes have in common is the need for an intermediary to enable them to bind to the fiber being dyed. In other words, when working with plants in this family, the mordanting stage is necessary.

2 · Quinones: a diversity of colors

Quinones, which are much less common in the plant kingdom than flavonoids, are interesting for the range of colors they offer, from the golden yellow-oranges of rhubarb and borage to cochineal pink, walnut brown, and the unmistakable rose madder.

Fungi, lichens, and insects contain quinone dyes. Among insects, the best-known sources of colorants are cochineal insects. Their use in textile dyes, paints, and food colorants is widespread and long-standing. Carminic acid and kermesic acid are present in abundance in the cochineal and in the lacquer resin produced by the insect. These dyes produce magnificent reds and pinks. Among quinone plants, it is mainly the roots that are interesting from a dyeing point of view.

The famous rose madder comes from alizarin, a dye found in the root of the rose madder plant. This dye is also found in other madder families, and more generally in all types of madder, but in lesser quantities.

For orangey yellows, turn to rhubarb and dock roots. These are resources that can easily be found in the vegetable garden or in the countryside. They have the added advantage of creating strong colors.

Less well-known, and reputed to be more fragile, the purple of alkanet roots is just as interesting for experimenting.

If, like me, you do not like digging up roots, you can turn to some local types of wood.

Young walnut shoots and their young leaves, rich in juglone, offer beautiful browns. And magnificent golden yellows can be obtained from borage and buckthorn bark.

Finally, henna powder is a fabulous color source for orangey reds. Lawsone, the colorant in henna, is of great interest in dyeing: a source of dye, it can also act as a reducing agent in the indigo vat (see p. 67).

All quinone plants generally have a good affinity with animal fibers.

3 · Tannins: from blacks, grays, and beiges to reddish-browns

As we have seen, tannins, by virtue of their chemical composition, have the ability to improve the affinity between the dye and the fiber to be dyed. As such, they can act as a mordant plant. But they can also be sources of color.

First, for black, we can refer to the experiment mentioned earlier: in the presence of iron, tannins immediately darken to grays or blacks.

Condensed tannins, particularly those known as proanthocyanidins, are true sources of color in their own right.

Some tannins can be sources of yellow, such as mastic and pomegranate bark.

Pinkish-browns can be obtained from the gum arabic tree; reddish-browns from other acacias such as catechu; and deep browns from chestnut bark.

The advantage of these color tannins is that they offer beautiful, strong tones without the need to mordant the fibers first.

4 · Indigo plants: blue, nothing but blue

There are many indigo-producing plants in the *Indigofera* genus, with the true indigo species (*Indigofera tinctoria*) being notable for its diversity and richness.

Cultivated or wild, these shrubs grow in Africa, Asia, India, and South America. They belong to

Artisan - FRANCE

the Fabaceae family of leguminous plants. These so-called pioneer plants have the particularity of fixing nitrogen from the air in the soil, making it available for other plants to assimilate. They make blue and fertilize the soil! What more could you ask for?

In northern latitudes, there is dyer's woad, also known as glastum (*Isatis tinctoria*), a biennial plant of the cabbage family (Brassicaceae). It grows wild in southern France and the Mediterranean, along roadsides, railroads, and meadows, and can also be found in western North America. This plant thrives in deep, well-drained clay-limestone soils. It loves warmth and sunshine. In the fifteenth and sixteenth centuries, woad cultivation was widespread in the South of France, particularly in the Lauragais area. Hence the expression *pays de cocagne* ("land of plenty"), referring to the abundance of crushed, dried balls of woad leaves known as *cocagnes*, marketed for indigo dyeing.

This crop is slowly making a comeback, thanks to the hard work of enthusiasts.

Another source of indigo blue that can be grown in northern climates is dyer's knotweed (*Persicaria tinctoria*, a member of the Polygonaceae family). Native to Vietnam and southern China, this herbaceous annual has become well established in Europe. It likes cool, well-watered soil. Enthusiasts of natural colors have also taken up knotweed cultivation for local indigo production.

There are other indigo plants, but they are more exotic and less well-known.

Particular mention should be made of a lovely Asian tree that offers light shade and a delicate fragrance: the harlequin glorybower tree (*Clerodendrum trichotomum*). In late summer, its flowers produce small turquoise-blue berries, which are loved by birds. These berries contain an indigo carmine derivative and can be dyed indigo blue only in boiling water, provided the berries are used fresh (see pp. 167–168).

All these plants do not contain indigo as such, but indigo precursors: molecules that, after a chemical reaction, produce the indigo pigment (see pp. 70–71).

Indigo plants are not used exclusively for color. In all indigo-producing cultures, these plants have also been used for their therapeutic virtues. As far back as antiquity, woad leaves were used as poultices to treat wounds, ulcers, and snake bites, and as a decoction to treat spleen ailments.

It was also customary to wear indigo-dyed textiles for protection against insects and snakes. The scent of indigo is said to have a repellent effect.

In traditional Chinese medicine, indigo plants are still used as medicinal plants. Renowned for its antiviral properties, in particular against the SARS coronavirus, Chinese woad saw renewed interest during the SARS epidemic in 2003. It also proves highly useful as an anti-inflammatory. It is traditionally used to treat mouth and lung ailments. Also known for its cleansing properties, it is said to relieve the liver and purify the blood.

Since 2011, woad has been included in the European pharmacopoeia. Today, this plant is the subject of numerous medical research projects for its anti-inflammatory, antitumor, antiviral, and antioxidant properties.

Lastly, a whole range of woad-based cosmetics are now being marketed for their skin-care benefits.

Where to find them?

Access to plant resources for dyeing is relatively easy.

In your kitchen, some of your plant waste can go into your saucepan instead of the compost bin: carrot tops, onion peels, banana or avocado skins, beet leaves, and more.

For larger quantities, contact a market gardener, grocer, or food retailer, who will be delighted to see their waste put to good use. Of course, I urge you to choose organically grown fruits and vegetables.

If you are lucky enough to have a garden, it is a great place to explore in search of color. You can grow so-called dye plants that are accustomed to cooler climates, such as madder, dyer's knotweed, sulfur cosmos, woad, weld, and many others.

Walks in the countryside or the forest can be an opportunity to pick a few wild plants, some of which are interesting from a dyeing point of view. Trees and shrubs provide an abundant source of plant material for dyeing. Making color with wild plants reveals the richness of biodiversity. Respecting it is essential to the practice of dyeing.

Wild foraging: harvesting without harming

A few rules are needed to ensure that any wild foraging does not harm biodiversity.

1. Only pick plants whose resources are abundant. Exclude protected or endangered species. If in doubt, you can identify the plant using the PlantNet app and refer to the threatened species in your area.
2. When picking, be careful not to trample neighboring plants and use clean tools to prevent any possible transfer of pathogens.
3. Pick only what you need, leaving at least a third of the plants in place to ensure their survival. Never pick isolated species.
4. It is preferable to pick a little in several places, always trying to ensure sustainability.
5. Leave some of the flowers and seeds so that the plant can be reseeded the following year.
6. Avoid uprooting plants, unless they are very common, such as dock.

The woody parts of a plant can be harvested with pruning shears or a pruning knife, while leaves can be cut with scissors. Flowers can be picked delicately with your fingertips.

If you are not going to use the plants you harvest right away, you will need to dry them.

Here are a few tips on how to dry your plants. Choose a dark, well-ventilated, dry place. An airy attic is ideal, provided the roof structure has not been chemically treated. Place the plants delicately on a drying rack, which you can buy ready-made or DIY with very little effort. You can find guides to building your own on the Internet. A few crates stacked one on top of the other with mosquito netting placed at the bottom of each one has allowed me to dry plants with ease. Large sprays of wild plants can be tied into bunches and hung upside down in a dry, dark place.

A plant can be considered dry when it crumbles with the tip of a finger, without feeling damp. It is then easy to grind into a fine powder.

If you intend to use your freshly harvested plants, remember to shake them well before proceeding. This is a useful way of getting all the plant's little inhabitants to leave their home.

For larger quantities, dried plants are available from herbalists. Online stores specializing in plant-based dyes also offer a wide range of dye plants, particularly those found in more temperate climates. You can choose them in the form of dried plant powder or plant extracts (very practical for tannins). In this way, you can complete your color palette with the richness of more exotic flora.

Water

We do not talk about water much, and yet it is essential because there is no dyeing without water. Water is required at every stage of the dyeing process.

Water quality

Water quality has a direct impact on dye quality. Its source, mineralization, and pH all influence the color obtained.

1 • Tap water

Tap water is easily accessible, but its quality varies depending on your area. In the absence of other sources, it can be used for dyeing, despite the (infinitesimal) dose of chlorine. Leaving the water to stand for at least one night and then heating it to boiling point will generally reduce the chlorine content considerably.

Be aware, however, that some plants will not like tap water if it is too hard. On the other hand, some plants will produce their best colors with hard water.

Not all tap water is created equal. I have experienced it myself: dyeing with logwood gave me a magnificent navy blue with city water from Lyon, while at home in the countryside, with the same

process and the same materials, I got a slightly purplish-blue. This variation is one of the quirks of natural dyeing.

For the fiber preparation and washing operations, there is no contraindication to using tap water. For the dyeing process itself, however, it is best to use rainwater.

2 · Rainwater

This is the water I prefer, as it is less mineralized and adulterated; on the other hand, it is less easily accessible.

If you live in a house, it is relatively easy to collect rainwater using rainwater harvesting tanks. Concrete and high-density polyethylene (HDPE) plastic tanks are the best for preserving water quality. Concrete tanks are renowned for neutralizing the natural acidity of rainwater.

If you cannot collect rainwater, you can instead use demineralized water, which is commercially available.

As for spring water, it is often loaded with mineral salts and therefore generally not suitable for natural dyeing. But I would be tempted, if I had the opportunity, to try out natural dyeing with ferruginous water.

Saving water

Let's face it—natural dyeing is water intensive, as the quantity of water required for a dye bath is significant. Generally speaking, the recommended ratio is 5 gallons (about 20 liters) to dye 2 pounds (about 1 kg) of fiber. For small quantities, this ratio is slightly increased: 1 gallon to dye 4.5 ounces (approximately the same ratio as 3 liters per 100 g).

These are mere guidelines. The important thing is ensuring that the fiber to be dyed is completely immersed in the bath without the bath being too diluted.

There are a few things you can do to limit your water consumption, or at least recycle it.

For example, I strongly recommend that you do not empty your dye and mordant baths until they are completely exhausted.

For dye baths, the color of the dye liquid is a good indicator: the clearer the water, the less dye the bath contains. Thus, baths can be used to make either lighter colors or overdyes to enrich the shades (see pp. 57–61).

For mordant baths, on the other hand, the color of the dye liquid is of no use. In fact, mordant baths tend to darken over time. The best way to know if they still work is to test them. Store leftover baths in airtight containers.

Once the baths have been used up, they can be recycled in the garden. Hydrangeas, for example, appreciate the end of baths made with symplocos, an alumina-rich plant that turns the flowers blue.

I empty my baths into my watering can after checking their pH. If the bath is rather acidic, I water plants that appreciate acidity, such as raspberry bushes and other red fruits. If, on the other hand, the bath is too alkaline, I correct it with vinegar before watering the garden plants.

All baths, whether a mordant or a dye bath, can be recycled in this way. And the garden benefits from it.

In the end, there is only one dye that is truly water saving: indigo. Once the vat has been assembled, if it is of a large volume, it will have great inertia. This means it can be kept for a long time, provided it is properly maintained. My vat, assembled in 2016, has never been emptied!

EQUIPMENT

The adventure of natural dyeing requires no special equipment when making colors for yourself. If you are equipped for cooking, then you will be equipped for natural dyeing.

It is generally advised that you have equipment dedicated exclusively to dyeing. This is true if you use alum, iron, or even lime for the indigo vat.

On the other hand, if you only use nontoxic plants with medicinal properties, this precaution is no longer as important.

Choose a well-ventilated place to work. Have some baking soda (sodium bicarbonate) or washing soda (sodium carbonate) on hand. A little chalk and lemon juice are always useful as well, depending on the recipe, as some plants are very sensitive to pH. Alkalizing or acidifying the bath allows you to play with the shades of color. Similarly, some plants, such as madder, do their best work in slightly hard water. As my water is rather soft, I always add a few pinches of chalk to my madder bath.

Pots

1 · Pot materials

The materials chosen must be "inert." In other words, they must not interfere with the composition of the dye bath.

- **Stainless steel** is the best choice. It is the most versatile and resistant material. Stainless steel is essential for preparing plant decoctions to extract mordants or colors.

- If you are hunting for secondhand dyeing equipment, you can easily find large **aluminum** stockpots. Stored in the kitchen, they can generally be a great help when you need to dye large quantities. Of course, they are not inert: a few milligrams of aluminum may migrate into your dye bath. These infinitesimal doses in a five-gallon dye bath will enhance the color at best, without risking pollution.

- As for **iron** or **copper** pots, they interact directly with the color by darkening or greening it. If you use them, be sure to stir constantly to avoid staining.

2 · Pot sizes

It is a good idea to choose different sizes: smaller saucepans for plant decoctions and larger stockpots for the dye baths. The volume of the dye bath depends on the weight of the fibers to be dyed. In general, 5 gallons of water are needed to dye 2 pounds of fiber (approximately 20 liters per 1 kg).

The capacity of your stockpot should therefore be suitable for the amount of fiber you wish to dye.

If you are dyeing skeins of yarn, choose pots that are taller than they are wide. Conversely, for fabrics, choose pots that are wider than they are tall so that the fabrics can be spread out to their full width.

Ideally, you should have pots of different sizes and volumes on hand to suit your specific projects.

Other equipment and utensils

In addition to the pots, you will need the equipment you usually find in a kitchen:

- gas or electric stove
- scale
- thermometer
- wooden spoons
- measuring spoons
- strainers
- cheesecloth for straining
- glass or stainless steel bowls for reserving the dye liquids
- plastic bowls and buckets
- gloves and apron

You should be able to find all the equipment you need for a fraction of the cost at secondhand stores and garage sales.

Finally, as you will see, it is important to control the pH of your preparations and adjust the level if necessary. That is why it is useful to have pH paper on hand as a measuring tool. This can be found in pharmacies. Even better, but much more expensive, is a pH meter. To adjust the pH level, lemon juice and baking soda or washing soda are always useful.

THE NATURAL DYEING PROCESS

At first glance, the process may seem a little complicated and time-consuming. Complicated? Not really: the steps are simple and rather repetitive.

Time-consuming? Certainly! Natural dyeing takes time. Sometimes, it might take several days. Picking, cutting, steeping, simmering, curing, simmering again, drying, washing, drying again: one step follows another. Each one needs its own time, a certain amount of time.

Try not to leave out any of the steps. Above all, patience and observation are essential before you see the color appear on the fiber, the magical moment when the plant alchemy takes place.

Weighing

Dry weighing the fibers to be dyed is the first step, the first reflex, before any dyeing project.

Knowing the weight of the fibers to be dyed enables you to determine:

- **the quantity of plants** you will need, whether for mordanting or coloring. In dyer's jargon, the plants are quantified as a percentage of the weight of fiber (WOF) to be dyed.

- **the volume of water** for the baths in which you will be immersing your fibers. Knowing how much water required for each bath will enable you to choose the right pot.

So far, nothing too complicated.

Preparing the fibers

Fiber preparation is an important step. It enables the fibers to better adhere to the plant's active ingredients, whether for mordanting or coloring.

This involves removing any possible treatments and other residues left on the fibers from when they were manufactured.

1 • Washing, scouring, scouring

Wool

A simple wash in lukewarm water (85°F/30°C) with a few drops of eco-friendly detergent is generally sufficient for wool.

For greasy wool, such as raw wool fleece or raw spinning wool (still coated with oil to facilitate spinning), wash with a gentle natural soap. Rinse thoroughly, always with lukewarm water to avoid temperature shock (risk of felting), until all soap residue has been removed.

Silk

If the silk is degummed, as is generally the case with manufactured silk, a simple wash with an eco-friendly detergent is all that is needed.

For raw silk, on the other hand, the preparation is more tedious. It is important to remove the sericin, the gum produced by the silkworm when it makes its cocoon, which is impervious to dyeing. To do this, the silk is soaked for an hour in a very hot bath (195–200°F/90–93°C) with a gentle natural soap. Add a tablespoon of washing soda to the rinse water. Here, too, rinse with care.

Plant fibers

All wax, pectin, and other treatments must be removed from the fibers. This is called "scouring."

Plant fibers should be washed at a high temperature (140–190°F/60–90°C) in water containing natural soap and washing soda. Use an amount of soap representing approximately 20 percent of the weight of the fiber to be washed and an amount of washing soda equivalent to 6 percent. Rinse thoroughly until the water runs clear. For more convenience, this can be done in the washing machine.

Some dyers use wheat bran baths to effectively clean cellulose fiber fabrics. Thanks to its high phosphate content, it dissolves all chemical residues.

Bran bath recipe:

- infuse wheat bran (½ cup per gallon or 20 g per 1 liter of water) at 85–105°F (30–40°C) in a cheesecloth tied into a pouch;
- knead the bran to a milky consistency;
- plunge the fibers into this water and knead for around twenty minutes to ensure they are fully soaked;
- take out the fibers, rinse thoroughly, wring out, and dry.

In principle, this step is unnecessary for **fibers marketed as "ready-to-dye."**

As for **antique linens**, they generally take color very well because the trials and tribulations of their past life—dirt of all kinds and the many washes with our grandmothers' soap—have polished them, giving them better adhesion to natural dyes.

2 · Pretreatment of plant-based fibers: animalizing fibers

As explained above, natural dyes "bind" better to protein-rich materials. The cellulosic nature of plant fibers makes this more difficult.

With this in mind, dyers the world over have devised recipes to make cellulose fibers more adherent to color by "enriching" them with proteins. This is known as "animalizing" the fiber.

To achieve this, dyers use local resources. The Japanese soak cotton in soy milk, while Indians bathe fabrics in a hot bath of sulfonated castor oil. The protein-rich milk of certain herbivores, such as sheep and goats, can be used in the same way.

I experimented with several processes—some already tried and tested, others not at all. One that caught my attention—because it is economical and local—was eggs. More specifically egg whites, which are very rich in protein (82 percent).

Here's how I do it, for 3.5 ounces (100 g) of plant fiber to be dyed:

- in a large bowl, break two egg whites;
- add lukewarm water and stir;
- plunge the fibers into this mixture so that they are well immersed and mix thoroughly. Add more water if necessary;
- heat in a double boiler for 1 hour at 120°F (50°C);
- allow the bath to cool;
- take out the fibers, wring and dry them in the sun;
- let cure for one to two days.

The fibers are then ready for further dyeing.

For a color that respects nature and the living world, I suggest you choose organic eggs.

If you need to prepare a large quantity of fabric, you can buy organic egg white powder, which is easier to use. In this case, the proportion is 10 percent of the weight of the fiber to be dyed.

This step, designed to animalize cotton or linen, is not essential. It is not practiced by all dyers. You can skip this step by mordanting with a highly effective aluminum acetate.

However, if you choose to mordant only with plants, the result is less effective for strong colors. That is why it is best to leave no stone unturned in order to optimize the dyeing process.

Mordanting the fibers with plants

The mordanting stage is not essential for all plants. Some plants offer colors called "substantive dyes": the dyes bind to the fiber without the need for an intermediary. I will introduce some of these plants in the recipes section.

For others, an intermediary is needed to attach the dye to the fiber.

In my quest for a fully plant-based dyeing practice, I have explored several plants that can replace alum or any other form of industrially produced aluminum.

Some are suitable for all fibers, others for only a few. Plants rich in oxalic acid are only suitable for wool and silk.

Similarly, I have found that certain mordant plants work best with certain dye plants. For example, yellow plants from the flavonoid family only work well with symplocos, as the dye needs the Al ion to reveal itself.

Finally, the mordanting strength of the different plants tested is also uneven. The best performer is symplocos, like all plants considered to be hyperaccumulators of aluminum. But it is not always readily available. So I looked for closer alternatives, which are always interesting to use if you want to highlight or recycle local resources. The downside is that a larger quantity of plants is needed for the mordanting to be effective.

As you can tell, mordanting with plants is not as simple and efficient as using alum powder. But I am not concerned with my process being efficient.

Making color for yourself using only plants is a more poetic and environmentally friendly gesture. You discover the richness of biodiversity. You look differently at what we call "plant waste" or so-called weeds, which as a source of color would be wrong to pass over.

The quest for plant mordants is a voyage of discovering biodiversity, a world full of colors.

I was able to sample the results of my tests, first with "the standard" tinctorial plants, then with lesser-known or less-usual ones, plants that you can easily glean from your local area.

Mordanting plants solely for use with animal fibers:

1 • Plants rich in oxalic acid

All plants rich in oxalic acid can be useful for mordanting animal fibers, both wool and silk.

It is found in the leaves of plants in the Polygonaceae family—docks, knotwee,.d s, rhubarbs—as well as in certain leaves of plants in the Amaranthaceae family—goosefoots, chards, and beets.

Among the Polygonaceae is **Japanese knotweed**. This unloved plant is a rich source of oxalic acid. Here is a good reason to reconcile with it.

Along roadsides and railroads, on industrial wastelands, in towns and the countryside, it is everywhere. Exuberant and incredibly vigorous, it is said to be "invasive." People are doing everything they can to get rid of it.

Yet it is the subject of much research. Its chemical compounds, particularly resveratrol, are attracting a great deal of interest in the medical research field. Its biomass is also being studied for composting. This plant loves metalliferous soils and is therefore recognized as a bioindicator of soils polluted by heavy metals, a property that can be put to good use in phytoremediation. This is one of the reasons why some people are wary of this plant, despite the fact that it is edible and a great source of honey.

Near my home in France, I can easily find it along the side of the road. I harvest the leaves at the end of summer. Bringing home an armful of flowering stems attracts all the bees in the garden, much to my delight as I watch them foraging. I allow the leaves to dry. Then I use them to mordant wool.

Beet tops, from the Amaranthaceae family, also contain a high concentration of oxalic acid. If you love beets and grow them in your vegetable garden, this is a great opportunity to recycle the tops for color.

Beets can be harvested throughout the summer, or even better at the end of the summer. Used fresh, immediately after harvesting, beet tops can offer deeper shades. However, if you cannot make a decoction right away, you can dry them. The results are still interesting.

If you do not grow beetroot, do not hesitate to ask your organic grower at the farmers market for beet tops, which usually end up in compost.

In any case, oxalic acid resources are in large supply, well diversified, and easily renewable. Your choice of plant will depend on your location and the season. The riper the plants, the greater the quantity of oxalic acid.

The leaves can be used fresh or dried. It is important to plan for the right amount of leaves: between 100 and 200 percent of the weight of the fiber to be dyed in the case of dry leaves, and between 400 and 500 percent for fresh leaves (these ratios are given as a guide).

Whatever the plant, the mordanting recipe is identical.

BEETROOT LEAF MORDANT

Beta vulgaris

Part used:
Aerial part, leaves, and stems

Quantity used:
Fresh leaves and stems: 400% of the weight of fiber to be dyed (WOF)
Dry leaves and stems: 100% of the weight of fiber to be dyed (WOF)
Dry-weigh the fiber to be dyed in order to determine the quantity of plants required

Extraction of mordant by decoction

1. Cut beet tops into small pieces with pruning shears or a pair of scissors. Place in a stockpot and cover with water—rainwater if possible.
2. Heat in a well-ventilated place. Gradually raise the temperature to a gentle simmer (190°F/ 90°C).
3. Stir regularly. Add water if necessary during cooking to compensate for evaporation and so that the plant remains submerged.
4. Continue simmering for 45 to 90 minutes.
5. Turn off the heat. Leave to cool.
6. Once cooled, strain the mordant liquid through a strainer and cheesecloth.
7. Reserve the mordant liquid.

- For a stronger concentration, you can make another decoction with the cooked plant material and add the second dye liquid to the first.

- If you worked with fresh leaves, you will obtain a bright pink liquid. This color is due to betalains, colorants found in most plant families belonging to the Caryophyllales order.

They are very bright but fragile dyes. They are therefore of limited use in natural dyeing. However, they work particularly well as food coloring.

Mordant bath

1 Pour the beet liquid into a pot large enough to allow the fibers to be dyed to spread out.
2 Add water—rainwater if possible—to obtain a ratio of approximately 2 lb of fibers to be dyed per 5 gallons (1 kg per 20 liters). Increase this ratio slightly for quantities of less than 3.5 ounces (100 g).
3 Submerge the prewashed, wrung-out fibers into the mordant bath. Spread them out well.
4 Turn on the heat and gradually raise the temperature to a gentle simmer (190°F/90°C).
5 Stir regularly and gently. Add hot water if necessary to keep the fibers fully submerged.
6 Simmer for 15 to 60 minutes, stirring regularly. The greater the quantity of fiber to be dyed, the longer the simmering time.
7 Turn off the heat and allow to cool.
8 Remove the fibers from the bath and wring them out to dry.

- Fibers cooked in the liquid of fresh leaves will have a pretty pinkish color, while those cooked with dry leaves will be yellowish. Mordant plants add subtle nuances to plant colors. Mordanting with fresh beet leaves goes very well with all pink and red plants.

- If your dyeing project is ready, you can then follow up with a dye bath with the plant of your choice. If not, let the beetroot leaf mordanted fibers dry and store them carefully for a later dyeing project.

---

2 · Birch

The inspiration for this recipe came from an old book by Louis-Alexandre Dambourney, an eighteenth-century French botanist and steward of the Jardin Botanique in Rouen, who was interested in using "indigenous" plants as a source of dye. His idea was to offer an alternative to the exotic tinctorial plants that were being used in large quantities at the time and were extremely expensive. He explored the local flora and experimented with an impressive number of plants. His experiments are recorded in his book *Recueil de procédés et d'expériences sur les teintures solides que vos végétaux indigènes communiquent aux laines et lainages*, which is freely accessible on the Internet. It is a wonderful journey back in time to the flora of the eighteenth century.

As was customary at the time, all the dyes he was able to obtain were made with metal mordants: alum, of course, but also copper, iron, and heavy metals such as tin, bismuth, and even lead. The question of their environmental impact was not on people's minds at the time.

Among all his experiments, one in particular that caught my attention used birch bark. *Betula pendula* is a pioneer tree that grows in abundance on forest wasteland in northern climes. After a multitude of trials, Dambourney was surprised to discover that birch bark could be used as a "mordant brightener" with logwood. My curiosity prompted me to try the experiment, but without a metal mordant.

Birch bark used on its own offers pretty shades of pink without the need for mordanting. That is its first benefit (for recipe, see p. 159).

But what interested me was its use as a mordant plant. The results were conclusive only on wool. As with most plant mordants—with the exception of symplocos—results are uneven for different dye plants. However, the alchemy between birch bark and logwood does indeed work. I did not get a blue (which is only possible in the presence of aluminum ions) but a pretty pinkish-violet: a shade worthy enough to retain birch bark as a mordant plant.

BIRCH BARK MORDANT

Betula alba

Part used:
Dried bark, ground or powdered

Quantity used:
100 to 200% of the weight of fiber to be dyed (WOF)
Dry-weigh the fiber to be dyed to determine the quantity of plant required

Extraction of mordant by decoction

1 Pour the bark into a stockpot and add water so that the plant powder is fully submerged.
2 Bring to a simmer, gradually raising the temperature to 190°F (90°C).
3 Add washing soda until the mixture reaches a pH of 8.
4 Stir regularly. Add water if necessary during simmering to compensate for evaporation and so that the plant remains submerged.
5 Maintain a gentle simmer for 60 to 90 minutes.
6 Turn off the heat. Allow to cool.
7 Strain the bath using a strainer and cheesecloth.
8 Reserve the mordant liquid.

- For a stronger concentration, you can repeat this step and make a second decoction. Add the second mordant liquid to the first.

Mordant bath

1 Pour the mordant liquid into a pot large enough to allow the fibers to be dyed to spread out.
2 Add water—rainwater if possible—to obtain a ratio of approximately 2 lb of fibers to be dyed per 5 gallons (1 kg per 20 liters). Increase this ratio slightly for quantities of less than 3.5 ounces (100 g).
3 Check the bath pH. Add washing soda if necessary to reach a pH of 8.
4 Add in the presoaked, wrung-out fibers to the bath. Spread them out well.
5 Turn on the heat and gradually raise the temperature to the simmering point (190°F/90°C).
6 Stir regularly and gently. Add hot water if necessary during the process to keep the fibers fully submerged.
7 Simmer for 15 to 60 minutes. The greater the quantity of fiber to be dyed, the longer the simmering time. Stir regularly throughout simmering.
8 Turn off the heat and allow to cool.
9 Remove the fibers from the bath and wring them out.

- The fibers will have taken on a pretty powdery pink color, which will have little influence on the final color.

- If your dyeing project is ready, you can follow up with a dye bath using the plant of your choice. Otherwise, let your mordanted fibers dry and store them carefully for a future dyeing project.

Mordant plants for plant fibers only: tannin plants

As I have already mentioned, tannins are an abundant and valuable resource in plant-based dyeing. Their ability to cling to cotton or linen fibers and attract natural dyes means that they have been widely used by artisans the world over to better fix color to fabric. Highly concentrated in hydrolyzable tannins, galls from trees such as oak, sumac, and many others were used as plant mordants, often combined with another mineral mordant for a stronger color. This use of tannins in the dyeing process is referred to as "galling."

Tannins can be used in various forms. The most readily available and free is to collect the leaves or twigs of tannin-rich plants such as black locust, chestnut, oak, sumac, alder, or pistachio. Since tannins are less concentrated in these plants than in wood, a good quantity of tannins should be used (at least 500 percent of the weight of the fiber to be dyed).

The most convenient method is using them in the form of an extract, whether walnut, chestnut, or sumac. You can find these in specialist stores selling plant dyes or extracts. Highly concentrated in tannins, they are normally used in small quantities. Nevertheless, for good adhesion, you should allow between 10 and 20 percent of the weight of the fiber to be dyed, depending on the quality of the extract.

RECIPE USING OAK, CHESTNUT, OR OTHER LEAVES RICH IN TANNINS

Part used:
Hardwood twigs

Recommended quantity:
Fresh leaves: 400 to 500% of the weight of the fiber to be dyed (WOF)
Dry-weigh the fiber to be dyed to determine the quantity of plants required

Extraction of mordant by decoction

1 Cut twigs into small pieces using pruning shears or a pair of scissors. Place in a stockpot and cover with water.
2 Turn on the heat and gradually raise the temperature to a gentle simmer (190°F/90°C).
3 Stir regularly. Add water if necessary during simmering to compensate for evaporation and so that the plant remains submerged.
4 Continue simmering for 45 to 90 minutes.
5 Turn off the heat. Leave to cool.
6 Once cooled, strain the mordant liquid through cheesecloth and a strainer.
7 Set mordant liquid aside.

- For a stronger concentration, you can make a second decoction with the leaves used the first time and add the second mordant liquid to the first.

- Once you have finished, you can compost the cooked leaves in the garden.

Mordant bath

1 Pour the plant mordant liquid into a pot large enough to allow the fibers to be dyed to spread out.

2 Add water—rainwater if possible—in order to reach a ratio of approximately 2 lb of fiber to be dyed per 5 gallons (1 kg per 20 liters). Slightly increase this ratio for quantities below 3.5 ounces (100 g).
3 Submerge the fibers (presoaked and wrung out) into the dye bath. Spread them out in the pot.
4 Turn on the heat and gradually raise the temperature to a simmering point (190°F/90°C).
5 Stir regularly and gently. Add hot water if necessary while simmering to keep the fibers fully submerged.
6 Simmer for 15 to 60 minutes. The greater the quantity of fibers to be dyed, the longer the simmering time. Stir regularly throughout.
7 Turn off the heat and allow to cool.
8 Remove the fibers from the bath and wring out to dry.

RECIPE USING EXTRACTS OF GALLNUTS OR OTHER TANNIN PLANTS

Recommended quantity:
Depending on the extract, 10 to 20% of the weight of the fiber to be dyed (WOF)
Dry-weigh the fiber to be dyed to determine the quantity of extract required

1 Pour the required amount of extract into a bowl and add boiling water.
2 Stir vigorously until the extract powder is completely diluted.
3 Pour the mordant liquid into a pot and add more water to prepare the mordant bath.

Follow the mordant bath steps in the recipe for fresh leaves (see pp. 42–45).

- The color of the mordanted fibers will depend on whether the tannins are hydrolyzed or condensed. The former are more or less colorless, while the latter contain colorants that will enhance the plant's own colorants. In this way, they enrich the shades that can be achieved.

- Once the fibers have been mordanted with tannin, you can use them immediately for a dyeing project after rinsing them. Otherwise, dry them for later use. Remember to rinse the fibers thoroughly before the dye bath.

Mordant plants for all fibers

1 • Symplocos

Symplocos is a hyperaccumulator plant of aluminum (see Mordant plants, p. 15). There are many varieties of symplocos. Most are acclimatized to tropical and subtropical climates. They are also medical plants used in Ayurvedic medicine.

My curiosity led me to plant a variety of symplocos acclimatized to temperate climates, *Symplocos paniculata*. Unfortunately, while still very young, it did not survive the exceptional drought of summer 2022.

Because of its high concentration of organic aluminum oxide, symplocos is one of the most effective mordant plants I have experimented with for replacing mineral alum, whether for animal or vegetable fibers.

It is effective with all dye plants. I particularly recommend it for yellow plants in the flavonoid family, such as weld or goldenrod, for striking, tangy yellows. With logwood, you can obtain a very distinctive navy blue on wool.

RECIPE USING SYMPLOCOS LEAF OR BARK

Symplocos cochinchinensis or *Symplocos racemosa*

Part used:
Depending on the symplocos variety, powdered leaves or bark

Recommended quantity:
20 to 50% of the weight of the fiber to be dyed (WOF)
Dry-weigh the fiber to be dyed to determine the quantity of plants required

Caution:
Symplocos does not like hard water. Use rainwater or fresh water, or purchase demineralized water.

Extraction of mordant by decoction

1 Pour the symplocos into a stockpot and add rainwater so that the plant powder is well submerged.
2 Turn on the heat and gradually raise the temperature to a gentle simmer (190°F/90°C).
3 Stir regularly. Add water as needed during simmering to compensate for evaporation and so that the plant remains submerged.
4 Keep simmering for 60 to 90 minutes.
5 Turn off the heat. Allow to cool.
6 Strain the bath using a strainer and cheesecloth.
7 Reserve the mordant liquid.

- For a higher concentration of aluminum oxide, you can repeat this step and make a second decoction. Add the second mordant liquid to the first.

- Once you have finished, you can compost the cooked symplocos leaves in your garden, especially at the bases of hydrangeas: they will appreciate it and offer you beautiful blue-tinged flowers.

Mordant bath

1 Pour the mordant liquid into a pot large enough to allow the fibers to be dyed to spread out.
2 Top up with water—rainwater if possible—to obtain a ratio of approximately 2 lb of fibers to be dyed per 5 gallons (1 kg per 20 liters). Increase this ratio slightly for quantities of less than 3.5 ounces (100 g).
3 Submerge the fibers (prewashed and wrung out) into the mordant bath. Allow them to spread out.
4 Turn on the heat and gradually raise the temperature to the simmering point (190°F/90°C).
5 Stir regularly and gently. Add hot water if necessary to keep the fibers submerged.
6 Simmer for 15 to 60 minutes. The greater the quantity of fibers to be dyed, the longer the simmering time. Be sure to stir regularly throughout.
7 Turn off the heat and allow to cool.
8 Remove the fibers from the bath and wring dry.

- Fibers mordanted with symplocos will have turned slightly yellow or pinkish-beige, depending on the variety used. These shades have little influence on the final color.

- After rinsing, the mordanted fibers can be used immediately for a dyeing project. Otherwise, dry them for later use. When making your project, remember to rinse the fibers well before the dye bath.

Tips for plant-based fibers

- For a deeper color in plant fibers, I recommend a technique used by Indian artisans: alternating galling and mordant baths. It is a bit tedious and time-consuming, but the result is a more saturated, longer-lasting hue.

- In concrete terms, after passing the fibers through a symplocos bath, wring them out and rinse them, then plunge them into a tannin bath (see Mordanting with tannin-rich plants, pp. 42–45). Simmer for about 20 minutes. Remove the fibers, wring them out, rinse, and plunge them back into the symplocos bath. Simmer for 20 minutes. You can repeat this process once or twice. The combination of aluminum ions and tannins will enhance the shade once dyed.

---

2 · Green tea leaves

Tea (*Camellia sinensis*) is a natural aluminum accumulator. The plant's ability to store Al ions in its leaves depends on several factors: soil geology, pH, climate, cultivation method, and harvesting period.

Studies on the composition of tea leaves show wide disparities in the concentrations of metals such as aluminum and iron in different tea samples.

Generally speaking, mature leaves, which correspond to the autumn harvest, contain more organic aluminum. This is the case with Bancha tea, a traditional Japanese green tea the Japanese people view as ordinary and consume daily. This is the tea I used for my tests. You can also use a classic, organically grown green tea. It will do the job just fine.

Tea's other chemical compounds are just as useful in the mordanting process. Its high concentration of flavonoids, particularly catechic tannins, will both color and coat the plant fiber to be dyed.

RECIPE USING GREEN TEA LEAVES

Camellia sinensis

Part used:
Whole or powdered leaves

Recommended quantity:
Dry leaves: 100% of the weight of fiber to be dyed (WOF)
Dry-weigh the fiber to be dyed to determine the quantity of plants required

Extraction of mordant by decoction

1. Pour tea into a pot and cover with water, rainwater if possible.
2. Turn on the heat. Gradually raise the temperature to a gentle simmer (190°F/90°C).
3. Stir regularly. Add water as needed during simmering to compensate for evaporation and so that the plant remains submerged.
4. Continue simmering for 45 to 90 minutes.
5. Turn off the heat. Leave to cool.
6. Once cooled, strain the mordant liquid through cheesecloth and a strainer.
7. Reserve the mordant liquid.

- For a stronger concentration, you can make another decoction with the leaves used the first time and add the second mordant liquid to the first.

- Once you have finished, you can compost the cooked leaves in your garden. Your garden will appreciate it.

Mordant bath

1 Pour the tea leaf mordant liquid into a pot large enough to allow the fibers to be dyed to adequately spread out.
2 Add water—if possible rainwater—to obtain a ratio of approximately 2 lb of fibers to be dyed per 5 gallons (1 kg per 20 liters). Increase this ratio slightly for quantities of less than 3.5 ounces (100 g).
3 Submerge the fibers (presoaked and wrung out) into the water. Spread them out well.
4 Turn on the heat and gradually raise the temperature to a simmer (190°F/90°C).
5 Stir regularly and gently. Add hot water as needed to keep the fibers submerged.
6 Simmer for 15 to 60 minutes. The greater the quantity of fibers to be dyed, the longer the simmering time. Be sure to stir regularly throughout.
7 Turn off the heat and allow to cool.
8 Remove the fibers from the bath and wring them out.

- The fibers will have taken on a slightly yellow color, due to the presence of flavonoids, such as quercetin, which will enrich the final color.

- If your dyeing project is ready, you can then follow up with a dye bath with the plant of your choice after rinsing the fibers. Otherwise, leave your mordanted fibers to dry and store them carefully for a future dyeing project.

---

3 · Banana peels

Using banana peels as mordant—what an idea! My curiosity and quest for completely plant-based color using renewable, sustainable, and easily accessible plant resources led me to experiment with this plant waste, with rather interesting results.

Everyone knows the banana plant for the edible use of its fruit. However, the plant as a whole—leaves and trunk—is valued for other uses in countries that grow them. As a considerable source of fiber, its biomass is recycled to make rope, textiles, and paper. In India and South America, banana sap is traditionally used to dye cotton. This last use caught my attention. Although there are hardy varieties of banana that can acclimatize to temperate climates, planting a banana tree in my garden seemed complicated. So I turned to the waste products I had on hand—banana peels—for my first attempts.

I was pleasantly surprised by the rather encouraging initial results. Since I was not trained as a scientist, I pursued my trials empirically, trying to understand how banana peels could serve as a mordant.

Over the course of my experiments, I have come up with a specific way of doing things. There is certainly room for improvement.

I found little information on the chemical analysis of banana peels. They are said to contain significant quantities of tannins, proteins, and other amino acids, including dopamine, as well as trace elements, such as potassium, in varying quantities. Banana peels are recommended for use in the garden as a fertilizer, in cosmetics for their softening and nourishing properties, and in herbal teas for their relaxing effects.

Here is another way to recycle banana peels by using them as a mordant to dye your fibers, wool, silk, cotton, or linen.

Because of their high tannin and protein content, banana peels are ideal for mordanting plant fibers. If you are in a hurry, you can even skip the fiber animalization and galling stages for a result that is still satisfactory.

Banana peel is an interesting mordant to combine with red plants, particularly madder. As for logwood, soaking the dyed plant fibers in an iron solution with added washing soda reveals a lovely blue.

RECIPE USING BANANA PEELS

Musa x paradisiaca

Part used:
Fresh, organically grown green or yellow banana peels, cut into small pieces

Recommended quantity:
100 to 200% of the weight of fiber to be dyed (WOF)
Dry-weigh the fiber to be dyed to determine the quantity of plant required

Extraction of mordant by decoction

1 Cut banana peels into small pieces using a pair of scissors or a knife. Place in a stockpot and cover with water—rainwater if possible.
2 Turn on the heat. Gradually raise the temperature to a gentle simmer (190°F/90°C).
3 Stir regularly. Add water as needed during cooking to compensate for evaporation and so that the plant remains fully submerged.
4 Maintain a gentle simmer for 45 to 90 minutes.
5 Turn off the heat. Allow to cool.
6 Once cooled, strain the liquid through cheesecloth and a strainer.
7 Reserve the mordant liquid.

- For a higher concentration, you can make another decoction with the cooked plant material and add the second mordant liquid to the first. Let the extract to mature for 24 to 48 hours.

- Once you have finished, you can compost the banana peels in the garden. Your garden will appreciate it.

Mordant bath

1 Pour the banana peel mordant liquid into a pot large enough to allow the fibers to be dyed to spread out.
2 Add water—rainwater if possible—to obtain a ratio of approximately 2 lb of fiber per 5 gallons (1 kg per 20 liters). Increase this ratio slightly for quantities of less than 3.5 ounces (100 g).
3 Submerge the prewashed and wrung-out fibers into the water. Spread them out well.
4 Turn on the heat and gradually raise the temperature to the boiling point (190°F/90°C).
5 Stir regularly and gently. Add hot water as needed to keep the fibers fully submerged.
6 Simmer for 15 to 60 minutes. The greater the quantity of fibers to be dyed, the longer the simmering time. Be sure to stir regularly throughout.
7 Turn off the heat and allow to cool.
8 Remove the fibers from the bath and wring them out.

- The fibers will have taken on a slightly pinkish-beige color, which should not influence the final color.

- Fibers mordanted with an extract prepared from dried banana peels take on a pretty pinkish color, but it is not as strong. For this reason, I recommend using fresh banana peels.

Dyeing the fibers

Once your fibers have been properly prepared and mordanted, it is time for the most magical and exciting part of the process: watching the plant's color gradually rise on the fibers.

Generally, this is done in two steps: first extracting the dyes from the plant, then the dye bath itself.

Dye extraction

The time frame for this step depends on whether you are working with plants you have harvested yourself or with dried plants or plant extracts purchased commercially.

For self-harvested plants, whether dried or fresh, you will need to cut them down to size so that they can release the maximum amount of dye. Using pruning shears, scissors, or even a food processor or grinder, chop up harvested plants as small as possible.

Berries and fruit should be crushed with a pestle and mortar.

Only flowers such as rudbeckia (black-eyed Susans) can be used whole.

In the case of commercially bought plants, whether from a herbalist or a store specializing in plant dyes, the dried plants will generally already be ground into chips or powder. They can be used in either form.

As for plant extracts, this is the most practical form. The extract is ready to use. Simply dissolve the extract powder in very hot water and stir vigorously until the powder is completely diluted. The recommended amount of extract is given by the manufacturer, generally 5 to 10 percent of the weight of the fiber to be dyed. Not all extracts are created equal. Their quality varies according to the way in which they have been manufactured, as well as how old they are. With experience, you will be able to judge for yourself.

To make your own plant extracts from dried or freshly cut or powdered plants, the extraction method may vary according to the plant. As with gardening, there are no universal rules, as each plant has its own specific needs. However, there are some general principles that can be adapted to suit each plant.

1 • The quantity of plants required

While there are no real standards, there are a few guidelines.

It is customary to say that for dry plants, the weight of plants should equal the weight of the fiber to be dyed.

This principle should be taken with a grain of salt, depending on the plant material used.

Some plants are very rich in dye. These include emblematic dyes such as logwood, sappanwood, and lac. In these cases, much smaller quantities (50 percent at most) can produce highly saturated colors.

On the other hand, for wild plants with lower dye content and for certain flowers that do not have a historical use for dyeing (and for good reason), higher quantities are required. Plan for at least 200 percent of the plant in relation to the fiber to be dyed, otherwise you will be disappointed by overly pale shades.

Therefore, when it comes to wild plants, choose ones that are common, sometimes considered invasive, such as Japanese knotweed, goldenrod, nettle, bramble, goosefoot, wild carrot, birch, black locust, pokeberry, and elderberry. These plants let you add color without harming biodiversity.

When you use fresh plants, which are often local, cultivated, or wild, they are naturally waterlogged. In this case, you need to significantly increase the quantity of plants. Allow for 400 to 600 percent of plants in relation to the weight of the fiber to be dyed.

2 • Method of extraction: decoction, maceration, or fermentation

Decoction

Most plants are extracted by decoction. Here is how to proceed:

- place plants in a stockpot;
- add enough water to cover the plants;
- turn on the heat and raise the temperature;
- add more water while simmering, if necessary, to compensate for the water evaporated and so that the plants remain submerged;
- stir regularly with a wooden spoon;
- turn off the heat and leave to cool;
- once the liquid is cooled, strain through cheesecloth and a strainer.

For a higher concentration of extract, you can make a second decoction with the plants you already used and pass it through the cheesecloth. This process is particularly useful for plants that are rich in dye but tough and hard, such as avocado skins, roots, wood chips, or wood powder.

The recommended simmering time and temperature, as well as the type of water, depend on the plant.

- **Cooking times**

  For soft plants, flowers, and leaves, simmering for forty-five minutes to an hour is sufficient.

  For wood and roots, on the other hand, the cooking time will be longer, from one to two hours, depending on the quantity of the plants.

- **Temperature**

  Some plants produce brighter colors if the temperature does not exceed 175°F (80°C). This is particularly true of madder root, which will turn brown if boiled.

  Similarly, some early-season herbaceous plants or leaves, such as nettle, fig leaves, and yarrow, can turn a soft yellow green if kept below the simmering point.

  But for tannin-rich plants, simmering is necessary for extraction. Similarly, hard plant parts such as bark and wood require a long decoction at a gentle simmer.

  The simmering time has an impact on the color obtained. You can see this for yourself: the color of your decoction will change as it cooks.

- **Water pH and hardness**

  This is an important criterion for certain plants.

  Rhubarb and turmeric, for example, will produce more vibrant yellows in a tangy decoction. In this case, add lemon juice during cooking to achieve a pH between 4 and 6. On the other hand, some plants do not like acidic environments: weld will be very pale, logwood will go brown, and madder turns orange.

  For this type of plant, adding washing soda during simmering will bring out its full potential. If your water is soft, a little chalk for lime-loving plants like madder will be beneficial.

  Experience has shown me how much the quality of the water can influence the shade of the plant color.

Maceration

To release the maximum amount of dye, some plants require maceration prior to decoction. This is particularly true of wildflowers, weld, madder root, sappanwood, and chestnut bark.

In a basin, pour warm water over the plants and soak overnight or even for two to three days. Over time, the water will become colored. You can then follow up with a decoction.

Fermentation

Unlike maceration, fermentation takes place in an acidic, oxygen-deprived environment, using rainwater.

Fermentation is a complex metabolic process. In plant dyeing, it can be a valuable resource for certain families of dyes. The yeasts and plant bacteria that develop in this particular environment essentially "digest" and transform the plant, thereby releasing colorant molecules. For this method, a gentle and continuous heat is required, hence the name "solar dyeing." It is a very energy-efficient extraction process and easy to implement in the summer.

This process is interesting for all plants rich in anthocyanins, such as berries, fruits, and flowers.

How to ferment dye plants:

- Fill a jar with plants: autumn berries or dark fruits, or dark flowers such as hibiscus, black hollyhock, or iris.
- Add a little white vinegar (8 to 14 percent). Some dyers recommend adding 10 percent salt, as for a brine. Personally, I do not use it.
- Seal the jar tightly with a rubber seal.
- Leave the jar in the sun for 3 to 10 days.
- Ensure that the temperature does not rise above 100°F (40°C).
- Regularly open the jar to let out gas and immediately close it again.

You can consider the fermentation complete when the liquid color is well satuated.

You can then filter the liquid and use it for dyeing, which also should be done at low temperatures (no more than 120°F/50°C) if it involves plants rich in anthocyanins. Excessive heat tends to degrade them.

Alternatively, if your jar is large enough, you can directly add your presoaked, wrung-out, and mordanted dyeing fibers into the jar. In that case, I recommend using animal fibers like wool or silk mordanted with a plant rich in oxalic acid.

THE DYE BATH

With mordanted fibers and colored plant extract, everything is ready for the moment you have been waiting for: dyeng your fibers.

1 Pour the plant extract liquid into a large stockpot whose size corresponds to the amount of water needed and the weight of the fiber to be dyed. add water, noting that 5 gallons of water are required for 2 lb of fiber to be dyed (20 liters per 1 kg). This is the dye bath. Start heating the bath.

- If you are dyeing skeins, they should be secured with figure eight ties in four places to prevent them from tangling. Your ties should be sufficiently loose but not too loose. Choose pots that are taller than they are wide. Conversely, if you are dyeing fabric, wider and shallower pots will be more suitable. This shape better allows the yardage to spread out correctly.

2 Wet the fibers in a basin of lukewarm water and immerse them in the dye bath. In the case of woven fabrics, it is important to make sure they are completely unfolded and dip them gently into the bath.

When the bath is very rich in dyes, the color rises very quickly on the fiber. That is why it is important to stir the fabric gently and regularly from the start to achieve a level (even) color.

3 Gradually raise the temperature, stirring regularly with a wooden spoon.

- The temperature, simmering time, and pH indications given for making an extract also apply to the dye bath. Thus, for a madder bath, the pH of the water should be at least 7, the water should be slightly hard, and the bath temperature should not exceed 175°F (80°C). For an onion peel bath, the pH should be around 8, the cooking time long and maintained at a gentle simmer (190°F/90°C). For a rhubarb root bath, the pH will be more acidic and the temperature will gradually rise to a simmer (190°F/90°C).
- Once again, everything depends on the plant's chemical composition: its colorants will express themselves more favorably in a certain environment, determined by pH, water quality, and bath temperature.

- A few precautions should be taken, however, depending on the nature of the fiber. Wool fears water that is too alkaline. I therefore recommend not adding too much base, such as washing soda, so as to keep the pH at 8 at most. Wool likes acidic environments. Plant fibers, on the other hand, tolerate high pH levels very well, making for an environment that is quite beneficial for dyeing.

- As far as temperature is concerned, wool, like linen, cotton, and other plant fibers, does not mind simmering as long as the temperature rise is gradual. Once again, wool is damaged not by heat but by the sudden transition from hot to cold. For silk, the temperature must not exceed 160°F (70°C), otherwise it will be damaged. Silk dyes very well in lukewarm or even cold water.

4 When you feel you have achieved the desired color, turn off the heat and allow the dye bath to cool.

5 Once the bath has cooled, remove the fibers and wring them out.

Your fibers are now dyed. At this point, you have two options:

- You are happy with the color and consider the dyeing process complete. In this case, dry your fibers away from the sun. Once dry, you can wash them.
- Or you would like to enrich or change the color. This is the finishing stage.

Finishes

This optional step is useful for enriching the palette of shades, either by overdyeing or soaking in iron water.

1 • Overdyeing

Overdyeing, which consists in applying a second dye bath, is particularly useful for obtaining shades of green.

In fact, few plants offer a direct green color. Red vine leaves can provide a soft green, provided they are picked early in the season and not heated above 160°F (70°C). Similarly, some wild herbs, such as nettle or yarrow, picked early in the season, can produce a tender green if heated below simmering point.

It is worth noting that producers of plant extracts now offer a chlorophyll extract made from alfalfa or mulberry leaves. Although it is expensive, it is effective and green. I have tested it with various mordant plants and obtained a relatively uniform green.

Beautiful, bold greens are possible with indigo overdyes. An initial color bath in a yellow plant followed by a dip in a vat of indigo offers a whole palette of greens. The shades will vary according to the plant used to make the yellow and how much indigo is in the vat.

The reverse is also possible: start with blue, then dye with a yellow plant. The shades of green will be different. The end of an indigo vat is a good way to modify your colors.

The second dye bath can be very lightly charged with dye for a gentle modification of the initial color that also makes for interesting practice. For example, you can obtain a variety of oranges by combining yellow and red plants.

This is why I advise you to keep your baths for some time before composting them: they can always be used to revive a color.

Let your creativity run wild as you string together leftover dye baths to finish. Like the walls of yesteryear, patinated by layers and time, your color will gain subtle and deep nuances.

However, there are a few precautions to keep in mind.

If you are dyeing wool, the indigo vat must be compatible with animal fibers (no iron vats). Similarly, the different dye plants must have the same pH affinities. For example, if you want to make a green with logwood, which hates acid baths, you will be better off choosing weld, which likes alkaline like logwood, rather than rhubarb, which tends to lose its luster if the bath is too alkaline.

In short, it is best to combine dye plants with identical needs.

2 • Modifying with iron

I recommend using iron only on plant fibers. Although wool and silk can tolerate a lightly dosed solution of iron acetate, which is less corrosive than iron sulfate, I prefer not to use it on animal fibers, as I do not want to risk damaging them. I therefore only use iron on plant fibers to soften a color or to turn it toward greens, black-grays, blue grays, or browns.

Iron reacts quickly and can leave permanent stains. Care must therefore be taken and only use utensils and containers intended exclusively for this use.

The reaction of iron with tannin-rich dye plants gives you a whole range of grays. Iron also acts on other dyes, making their hues greener. With certain plants, you can obtain beautiful shades of blue.

- **Making iron water**
  Pour 2 cups of white vinegar (preferably 14 percent) in a jar and add a piece of steel wool, iron nails, or even iron filings, made of oxidizable iron. Add water to top off the jar, if necessary. Close the jar. After a week or so, you'll have a liquid that will turn orange over time. This is iron acetate. You can use a little of the liquid to make your new shade.

- **Modifying with iron water**
  Simply soak the fibers in iron water taken from the jar. Add water so that the fibers are fully submerged. Wear gloves when handling the fabric. Be attentive, as the shade changes very quickly, usually in just a few minutes. Remove the fabric as soon as you have achieved the desired color. Rinse immediately with clean water and dry in the shade.

  The higher the iron content of your iron acetate solution, the faster the color will change.

3 • Washing

Washing is the final stage.

It is time for that recurring question for all those experimenting with plant-based color: does the color hold up in the wash? If a few precautions are taken (see Washing tips, p. 61) and if all the steps have been followed correctly, the plant color will stand up to washing.

But before you start dyeing with plant-based dyes, you should be aware that, over time and depending on the durability of the dye, which varies from plant to plant, some shades may fade a little, in the same way that a synthetic, petroleum-based color loses its brightness after a few washes.

Making plant-based color is a full-fledged approach with your heart open to plants. Through this practice, you learn a lot from them. With time and experience, you will choose plants according to the textile use of the fibers to be dyed. For fabrics that will be subjected to harsh conditions, such as UV rays and frequent washing, choose plants renowned for their colorfastness and add tannin plants, which are very effective for improving colorfastness.

In any case, if the color has faded, there is nothing to stop you from redyeing your textile with the same plant, or another plant to modify the color. This is what I do regularly: a new dye bath just for the pleasure of changing the colors in my wardrobe.

- **Washing tips**

Particular attention should be taken with the quality of the water and detergent used.

Washing should be done in pH-neutral water. This is generally the case with tap water. As explained earlier, depending on the plant, the water's pH can interact with the color. That is why I advise you not to use white vinegar, washing soda, or soda-based detergents. An eco-friendly detergent (soap-free if possible) for delicate fabrics is fine. A few drops of soap-free organic baby shampoo work very well on wool.

When it comes to temperature, take special precautions with wool. Hand wash in lukewarm water (85°F/30°C). No need to scrub, as this will damage the fibers. Just let the wool soak for a few minutes, then rinse with water at the same temperature (lukewarm). Thermal shock from hot to cold damages the wool and can lead to felting. Wring out the wool in a terry towel and dry.

As for plant fibers, which are more resistant, machine-washing poses no problem with a suitable eco-friendly detergent.

Plant color may bleed in the wash, particularly with certain plants rich in colorants. This phenomenon is normal and has no influence on the quality or durability of the dye.

What can be more problematic is if the color does not hold in the wash, a sign that the mordanting process may not have been sufficiently effective, the fiber may have been poorly prepared, or the plant extract may have been too low in dyes. As plant fibers are less apt to take dye, you are likely to experience this kind of disappointment with this type of fiber. You can always make another dye bath or treat the fiber with iron water.

SUMMARY OF THE STEPS AND ACTIONS ESSENTIAL TO THE DYEING PROCESS

■ For all fibers
■ For plant fibers only
■ For animal fibers only

STEP 1 • WEIGHING

■ Dry-weighing the fibers to be dyed is the first essential step. This weight determines the quantity of plants required for the various dyeing stages, as well as how much water is needed for the mordant and dye baths.

STEP 2 • PREPARING THE FIBER

■ WASHING
Depending on the nature and quality of the fiber, simple washing (wool), degumming (raw silk), or scouring (vegetable fiber) is recommended.
Not necessary for "ready-to-dye" fibers.

■ "ANIMILIZING" THE FIBER
This optional step improves the affinity of cellulose fibers with vegetable dyes. Soak fibers in warm water enriched with protein, such as soy milk, sheep's milk, or egg white.
Allow fibers to air-dry.

STEP 3 • MORDANTING THE FIBER

A two-step process. Optional for plants with substantive color.

1 • MAKING THE PLANT-BASED MORDANT EXTRACT

■ The choice of plant will depend on the plant resources available and/or the nature of the fiber to be dyed.

■ "Universal" mordant plants: symplocos, green tea, banana peels.
Plants rich in oxalic acid: rhubarb, beet, dock, or Japanese knotweed leaves.
Birch bark.

■ Plants rich in tannins: gallnuts, tara, sumac, chestnut, or cachou.
For deeper color, alternate tannin baths with symplocos or aloe vera baths.

2 • PLANT-BASED MORDANT BATH
Ratio of water required for the bath: 5 gallons of water for 2 lb of fiber to be dyed (20 liters per 1 kg). Increase the ratio for small quantities (between 3 and 7 ounces/100 and 200g). The presoaked fibers are plunged into the mordant bath, ensuring that they can sufficiently unfold. Heat the bath and gradually raise the temperature. Stir regularly throughout the simmering process. Wring out the fibers and leave them to dry. They can be stored for later use or rinsed for immediate use. For silk, the mordant bath should be cold.

STEP 4 • DYE BATH
This is a two-step process.
1 • MAKING THE DYE PLANT EXTRACT
Obtained by decoction. Simmering time and temperature depend on the part of the plant used: flowers, leaves, wood, or roots. For some plants, extraction at an alkaline pH will be necessary.
2 • PLANT-BASED DYE BATH
Ratio of water needed for bath: 5 gallons of water for 2 lb of fiber to be dyed (20 liters per 1 kg). Increase the ratio for small quantities (between 3.5 and 7 ounces/100 and 200 g). Depending on the plant, the bath will be either acidic or alkaline. The presoaked fibers are plunged into the dye bath, ensuring that they have enough room to spread out. Heat the bath and gradually raise the temperature. Stir regularly throughout the simmering process. Wring out the fibers.

STEP 5 • MODIFICATION
Optional step that either modifies the color or enriches the shade.
MODIFYING THE COLOR WITH IRON Soak fibers in iron water. Once the desired shade has been achieved, rinse with clean water. ENRICHING THE SHADE Dip wet, wrung-out fibers either in the remains of another dye bath, for a deeper color, or in a vat of indigo, for shades of green or purple.

STEP 6 • WASHING
Once dyeing is complete, wash the dried fibers away from the sun, preferably with a neutral pH. Choose eco-friendly, soap-free detergents if possible.

INDIGO:
A DYEING PROCESS ALL ITS OWN

What is indigo? A color, you might say. Indigo blue, a color we all recognize.

A color with a long history. Unloved in antiquity, it was the color of barbarians and foreigners. Today, in Western cultures, blue is the preferred color, the color of consensus. Blue jeans, a cotton fabric dyed with indigo, are a major contributor to this trend. According to historian Michel Pastoureau, "it is the most reasonable color of all," chosen to embody harmony and freedom. But it is all a matter of culture and history.

This color is loaded with so many symbols, and it is certainly also because, from time immemorial and in almost every place, people have made blue, thanks to indigo.

Indigo is not a plant but an organic extract from plants, which, after multiple chemical reactions, directly dyes fibers blue, a light- and wash-resistant blue. It is said to have been discovered accidentally: an herbal tea made from plants belonging to the *Indigofera* genus, which supposedly produced pretty blue bubbles with a greenish liquid, may well have marked the beginning of the history of indigo dyeing.

Indigotine, an insoluble color

In the world of natural dyes, indigo is usually distinguished from other dyes. There are at least two reasons for this.

Firstly, indigo is a dye that does not need a mordant. In other words, there is no need to mordant the fiber to be dyed. Indigo has a direct affinity with the fiber. But this is not what makes it special, as other plants can be used to make color without mordanting (including avocado p. 106, onion p. 111, and turmeric p. 114).

Indigo is distinguished from all other dyes by two unique characteristics.

Firstly, indigo does not exist as such in so-called indigo plants. In fact, these plants contain molecules called "indican" and "isatan B," both glycosides that, following a chemical reaction involving grinding, maceration, and oxygenation, produce another chemical compound, the indigo pigment. Chemists refers to indican and isatan B as "indigo precursors."

The other particularity, and not the least, is that the indigo resulting from this reaction is a pigment, not a dye. Unlike a dye, which is soluble in water, a pigment is insoluble, remaining suspended in a liquid. Indigo pigment needs to be solubilized so that it clings to the fiber to be dyed. To make it soluble, it must undergo a further transformation through a chemical reaction in a vat, creating a basic, low-oxygen environment. Indigo is thus referred to as a "vat" dye. I will come back to this later.

To put it simply, we can summarize as follows. When it comes to dye plants, water-soluble dyes are extracted from them by decoction: quercetin for onions, luteolin for weld, and alizarin for madder. These molecules color the water in the bath in which the fibers to be dyed are immersed. This is the principle of the dye bath.

As for indigo plants, the pigment is extracted from them through a process a little more complex than a simple decoction. This intensely blue indigo pigment, also known as "indigotine" or "indigo carmine," is made soluble in an alkaline, oxygen-reduced vat. This is the indigo vat. Simply soaking the fiber to be dyed in this vat, followed by exposure to air, is all it takes to dye it blue.

That is what makes indigo so magical! Starting with green leaves, after a succession of chemical reactions involving the transformation of this plant material, indigo blue fabric is obtained almost instantaneously by soaking. The most famous blue of all time.

That is why there is such a buzz around indigo: it is surprising and mysterious. Who would have thought that a plant with pretty yellow flowers from the cabbage family, the woad (*Isatis tinctoria*), could conceal this blue gold in its leaves?

How can indigo pigment be extracted from the leaves of indigo plants?

There is a vast amount of literature on the subject, detailing ancestral know-how that varies according to the plant used. Some of these techniques are very elaborate, such as Japanese indigo, a compost of indigo leaves skillfully dosed to obtain an indigotine concentrate. I will only mention the best-known processes here.

Extraction of indigo by maceration

The simplest process, and certainly the first tried and tested, is based on fresh knotweed or woad leaves.

Ethnologist Anne Varichon details the steps involved: "To dye 500 grams [just over 1 lb] of wool, silk, linen, or cotton: scald 500 grams of fresh leaves with 4 liters [1 gallon] of water and let the temperature drop to 50°C [120°F]. Stabilize for a day. Enzymes present in the leaves and secreted by bacteria also present on the leaves cause hydrolysis of the precursors. When bubbles appear on the surface of the bath (a sign of fermentation), add 6 grams [1 ½ tsp] of slaked lime and stir, maintaining the temperature at 50°C [120°F] for an additional three hours. Finally, introduce the wet cloth, keep it immersed for a few minutes, take it out, and spread it out in the air. Repeat until the desired shade is achieved."

If you have a bit of woad growing near you, it might be fun to try the experiment, which is very accessible, and have blue at your fingertips.

Although it was simple to implement, the process was soon abandoned because of its disadvantages: very pale blues and long, repeated soaking times.

Other, slightly more elaborate extraction processes were soon devised, allowing dyers to obtain a higher concentration of indigo.

Extraction of indigo by composting

This process has existed since antiquity and continues to this day. The leaves are crushed, dried, and composted. They are then shaped into balls, called *coques* or *cocagnes* in French, then into the *agranat*, to facilitate marketing. In Japan, a similar process is used with purple knotweed leaves, known as *sukumo ai*.

The composting process concentrates the organic matter and extracts the indigo thanks to the work of microorganisms that form a veritable indigo yeast.

Today, this method is practiced by master indigo dyers, who perpetuate their ancestral know-how.

There is one final pigment extraction process, discovered in the eighteenth century and used today by most indigo producers: a process using fresh leaves, which is simpler and faster than composting and yields indigo that is just as concentrated.

Extraction by precipitation

Freshly harvested leaves are macerated in large vats of hot water. The infusion is collected and filtered, then beaten in order to be oxygenated with a little lime. This oxygenation precipitates indoxyl, the precursor present in the plant's liquid, into indigo flakes. The indigo pigment settles at the bottom of the vat, as it is insoluble. It is then filtered and dried. The indigo pigment you find as a blue powder on the market has been extracted in this way.

All that remains is to make the indigo pigment soluble so that it can be dyed. This is the indigo vat stage.

The indigo vat: a fermentation medium to make indigotine soluble

Solubilizing the indigo pigment is a necessary and essential condition for dyeing. There are all kinds of indigo vat recipes. Every master dyer specializing in indigo has their own secrets, their own knowledge acquired through experience. Because when it comes to indigo, recipes aren't everything. It guides us in our first steps, and then experience and observation enable us to move forward, sometimes by trial and error, but always making progress.

An indigo vat is a bit like yeast for bread-makers or a mash for beer brewers: it is alive. You get to know it by sight, smell, and, for some, even taste.

Despite their diversity, all vat recipes have two essential conditions for transforming indigo pigment into indigo dye.

- an alkaline environment
- an oxygen-reduced environment

The environment must be alkaline, i.e. with a pH between 9 and 12. This can be achieved with potash, washing soda, or lime. For convenience, we will use slaked lime.

It is also an environment in which oxygen has been eliminated by using a reducing compound. For natural vats, I suggest two types of reducing agent: a metallic one, iron, and a vegetable one, sugar (fructose) or henna. But there are many others.

Assembling an indigo vat

There are several indigo vat recipes. Here you will find the recipes that I use, which I think are relatively simple. My advice is therefore not "gospel," but based on my own experience.

I suggest you use two types of vat:

- a hot vat for all fibers, made with henna or fructose
- a cold vat for plant fibers only, made with iron

These are eco-friendly and natural tanks.

Quantities: two rules to remember

Generally, in natural dyeing, the quantity of plants is determined by the weight of the fiber to be dyed (WOF). With indigo, it is the amount of water in your vat that determines the quantity of indigo.

The principle to remember is: ½ to 1 teaspoon (approximately 3 to 5 g) of indigo for 1 quart (about 1 liter) of water. For a 1.3-gallon (5-liter) vat, you will need 3 teaspoons (15 g) of indigo. If you want very deep blues, you can increase the dose to 4 teaspoons (20 g). The water in the vat is ordinary water—tap water is fine.

The quantity of indigo determines the quantity of the other components in the vat.

As taught by master dyer Michel Garcia, with whom I studied, there is a simple mnemonic: "1, 2, 3." In other words:

- one part indigo;
- two parts lime;
- three parts reducer.

The recipes I am about to give you are for a 1.3-gallon (5-liter) vat, the smallest you can make. However, the larger your vat, the longer it will last, thanks to its force of inertia.

By applying these rules, you will be able to make larger vats yourself.

Equipment

- scale
- measuring spoons
- thermometer
- pH paper
- small plastic bucket or other glass container (minimum capacity 2 quarts/2 liters) with a tight seal
- large plastic bucket
- for a hot vat, equipment to heat it in a double boiler or a stainless steel container taller than it is wide (minimum capacity 5 quarts/5 liters)
- stovetop or cooktop
- wooden spoon and stick
- plastic basins or buckets
- stainless steel pot or stockpot
- strainer and cheesecloth
- gloves and apron
- rack

Ingredients

For all recipes:

- indigo pigment in powder form
- slaked lime (available in home improvement stores)
- washing soda (sodium carbonate) or baking soda (sodium bicarbonate)
- white vinegar

Depending on recipe:

- fructose for a fructose vat
- henna powder (*Lawsonia inermis*) for a henna vat
- iron sulfate (green powder) for an iron vat

Henna vat

For a 1.3-gallon (5-liter) vat:

- 1 ⅓ tsp (20 g) indigo pigment
- 2 ⅔ tsp (40 g) slaked lime
- 4 tsp (60 g) henna

1 Make a decoction of the henna in a stainless steel stockpot with 6 cups (1.5 liters) of water. Boil for at least 10 minutes, until the plant falls to the bottom of the pot.
2 Meanwhile, heat 4 or 5 quarts of water in a plastic bucket heated over a double boiler (place a cloth under the bucket as a precaution) or in a stainless steel stockpot. At 160°F (70°C), turn off the heat.
3 Pour the indigo and lime into a small sealable container (plastic or glass). Close tightly and shake vigorously for a few minutes to mix well, a bit like maracas.
4 Strain the hot henna decoction and pour it directly and gently into the lime-indigo mixture. Stir gently with a wooden spoon.
5 Carefully pour the resulting liquid (dark blue on the surface, yellow underneath) into the indigo vat, previously heated to 160°F (70°C). To prevent oxygen from entering, bring the container up to the edge of the vat and pour gently. If any sediment remains at the bottom of the container, add hot water and repeat.
6 Use the wooden stick to mix the bowl like a centrifuge, swirling the center of the bowl.
7 Let stand. Repeat step 6 two or three times.
8 Look for the signs that the vat is ready: blue bubbles in the center (the "bloom"), greenish-yellow liquid, and a coppery surface.
9 Leave the vat to stand overnight before dyeing.

Fructose Vat

For a 1.3-gallon (5-liter) vat:

- 1 tbsp (15 grams) indigo pigment
- 2 tbsp (30 grams) slaked lime
- 3 tbsp (45 grams) fructose

1 Mix all ingredients in a small sealable container (plastic or glass). Close tightly and shake vigorously for a few minutes to mix well, a bit like maracas.
2 Meanwhile, heat 4 quarts (4 liters) of water in a plastic bucket heated in a double boiler (put a cloth under the bucket as a precaution) or in a stainless steel stockpot. At 160°F (70°C), turn off the heat.
3 Heat 1 quart (1 liter) of water in a kettle until it boils. Gently pour the hot water into the indigo-lime-fructose mixture. Stir gently with a wooden spoon.
4 Follow steps 5 to 9 of the henna vat recipe.

Iron Vat

(For use with vegetable fibers only)
For a 1.3-gallon (5-liter) vat:

- 1 tbsp (15 grams) indigo pigment
- 2 tbsp (30 grams) slaked lime
- 3 tbsp (45 grams) iron sulfate

1 Mix all ingredients in a small sealable container (plastic or glass). Close tightly and shake vigorously for a few minutes to mix well, a bit like maracas.
2 Meanwhile, heat 4 quarts (4 liters) of water in a plastic bucket heated in a double boiler (put a cloth under the bucket as a precaution) or in a stainless steel stockpot. At 120°F (50°C), turn off the heat.
3 Heat 1 quart (1 liter) of water in a kettle until it boils. Gently pour the hot water into the indigo-lime-iron sulfate mixture. Stir gently with a wooden spoon.
4 Follow steps 5 to 9 of the henna vat recipe.

Steps for indigo dyeing

Remember to assemble your vat the day before you plan to dye. It will be all the better for it.

To begin, if you are using a henna or fructose vat, heat the vat to 140°F (60°C). Turn off the heat. If you are using an iron vat, there's no need to heat it—it is done cold.

Stir with a wooden stick, like a centrifuge. Leave to rest. Repeat twice.

The vat is ready for use if:

- there's a pretty blue bloom and blue bubbles in the center;
- the liquid in the tank is green, or even greenish-yellow;
- the surface of the tank is coppery, with a shiny appearance that breaks when you touch the surface.

These are the signs of a good vat in which the indigo pigment has been dissolved.

Using the pH paper, you can check the pH of the vat, which should normally be around 11.

A final recommendation: gently place a grid at the bottom of the vat to prevent the fibers from coming into contact with lime deposits.

Now you are ready to start dyeing!

Indigo dyeing techniques

1 Test first: dip a small square of wet, wrung-out fabric into the vat for two minutes. Take it out, shake in the air and rinse immediately. If the blue color, although light, holds, the vat is good.
2 Wet the fibers to be dyed in a basin of warm water. Wring them out well.
3 Gradually plunge the fibers vertically into the vat, taking care not to let any air in. In the case of fabric or clothing, spread them out to avoid wrinkles and air bubbles.
4 Soak for 3 minutes.
5 Take the fibers out just as gently, and press them just above the vat, always taking care not to add oxygen to the vat.
6 Spread out the fibers, which will gradually turn from greenish to blue. On contact with air, the indigo reveals itself as it oxidizes and clings to the fiber.
7 Leave to air out for about 10 minutes.

Repeat steps 4 to 7 several times, increasing the soaking time with each repetition: five minutes, then ten minutes, then twenty, thirty, or even forty-five minutes.

These times are given only as a guideline.

Remember to dip your hands, gloved or not, into the vat each time you soak, and to always stir the fibers gently as you do so that they soak evenly.

Successive soaking followed by oxidation (exposure of the fibers to air) will strengthen the blue and reduce any mottling. This is known as the "degreening" process.

Proceed in this way until the desired shade is obtained. Bear in mind, however, that the shade will be lighter once the fiber is dry, especially on plant fibers.

To finish, leave the dyed fibers to dry in the open air, hanging on a line, for at least twenty minutes, in order to allow the indigo to oxidize. I usually leave them longer, as I am often busy with other things.

Tips for dyeing wool

Wool does not like bases, which tend to make the fibers rougher.

That is why I advise you to start dyeing with plant fibers when the pH of the vat is at its highest, and only dye wool when the pH has decreased. A pH of 9 is ideal for animal fibers.

Rinsing and washing

Fill a basin with warm water and add a good amount of white vinegar: to give you an idea, for 5 gallons (20 liters), I pour at least a third of a 1-quart (1-liter) bottle.

Dip in the dyed fibers and mix. This removes any excess lime. It gives off a rotten-egg smell. This is a good sign. The shade of blue will strengthen further and continue to develop over the next few days.

For wool, take care to avoid thermal shock, otherwise felting will occur.

Allow to dry.

Wait one day for the color to set deeply.

Wash with an eco-friendly detergent until the water runs clear.

Wring out and dry, but not necessarily out of direct sunlight. Indigo is known for its UV protection.

Tips for maintaining your vat

When an indigo vat has worked well, it tends to be oxygenated by successive dips and the pH lowers as a result. Conditions are then no longer favorable for the indigo vat to function properly.

What are the signs of an "unhealthy" vat?

There are four indicators of vat health. They should be checked after stirring the tank three times, with pauses in between. This is called "waking up" the tank.

1 · Tank pH
If the pH is below 9, it needs more lime. The ideal pH is 11.

2 · Liquid color
It should be green, a sign of good reduction. If it is gray or bluish-black, it needs more base and reducer.

3 · Copper skin
A coppery film on the surface of the vat is a sign of a perfectly healthy vat. If only this film is missing, a reducer should be added.

4 · Bloom color
If the bubbles in the center of the vat are pale blue, it needs more indigo.

How do you maintain a "healthy" tank?

A few preventive precautions should be taken when using your tank.

After each dyeing session, sprinkle the vat with a little sugar, or with iron sulfate dissolved in a little hot water in the case of an iron vat.

If possible, cover the vat with a tight-fitting lid to prevent oxygenation.

Before each dyeing session, sprinkle with a little lime. Then heat the vat, in the case of a henna or sugar vat.

If the bloom remains pale, refill the vat. Alternatively, make a vat in very small batches, as indicated in the recipes, and pour it gently into the vat. Stir and wait a few minutes before dyeing again.

The larger the vat, the greater the inertia and the slower the degradation.

Some vats can be kept for a very long time. With experience, you'll learn to understand your vat.

PART 2

THE QUEST FOR COLORS: RECIPES AND INSPIRATIONS

Once you understand the steps involved in the dyeing process, all you have to do is gather up some kitchen equipment and get started making your own fully plant-based colors.

To guide you in your first steps, in this section you'll find some recipes I've experimented with using local dye plants. They are listed according to where you can glean these plant resources: in your kitchen or vegetable garden, in the flower garden, or on your walks through the countryside or the forest.

This is just a snippet of the plants you can use to create color. I can only encourage you to explore other paths and experiment, if you have not already done so, with other plants.

Experience will teach you a great deal. Over time, you will become more confident in your technique, and your eye will become sharper at picking out the subtle nuances that plant colors have to offer.

You will sometimes be disappointed, but you will also make some wonderful discoveries. Whatever the outcome of your experiments, I hope that the special alchemy of plant color will give you a dose of wonder.

All recipes indicate:

- **a quantity of plants**. It is expressed as a percentage of the weight of the fiber to be dyed (WOF). This ratio is a guideline. You are free to adapt it according to your resources or desired shade.

- **temperature and simmering time**. Depending on the plant, I generally distinguish between two temperatures: below simmering (175°F/80°C) and low boiling (between 185–195°F/85–90°C). You need to be careful with the former. Simmering times are given as a guide only. Of course, the length of time depends on the quantity of plants and fibers you are dyeing. The larger the quantities, the longer the heating time. You do not have to follow the time indicated to the letter. You can turn off the heat when you are satisfied with the shade you have achieved. Just bear in mind that on plant fibers, colors will lighten as they dry.

- **a quantity of water for the dye bath**. The ratio of 5 gallons (2 liters) of water to 2 lb (1 kg) of fiber to be dyed should be adapted to your project (see Water, p. 26).

IN THE FLOWER GARDEN: CULTIVATED PLANTS

The multitude and diversity of colors of summer flowers in the garden arouse the curiosity of the budding dyer, secretly dreaming of being able to "fix" these luminous colors on wool yarn or fabric.

I cannot help but invite you to give it a try. You may be pleasantly surprised. Most of these flowers are rich in flavonoids, from the yellow family. Marigolds, tickseeds, and yellow cosmos offer a beautiful palette of yellows and oranges.

Other flowers contain anthocyanins, a special colorant in the flavonoid family, which can give you magnificent pink or blue-violet hues, including purple hollyhocks, blue or purple irises, and rudbeckia.

Here is an overview of the flowering plants I have grown in my garden. But there are plenty of others to experiment with. I will also look at two well-known emblematic dye plants that can be grown in the garden.

Sulfur cosmos

Cosmos sulphureus

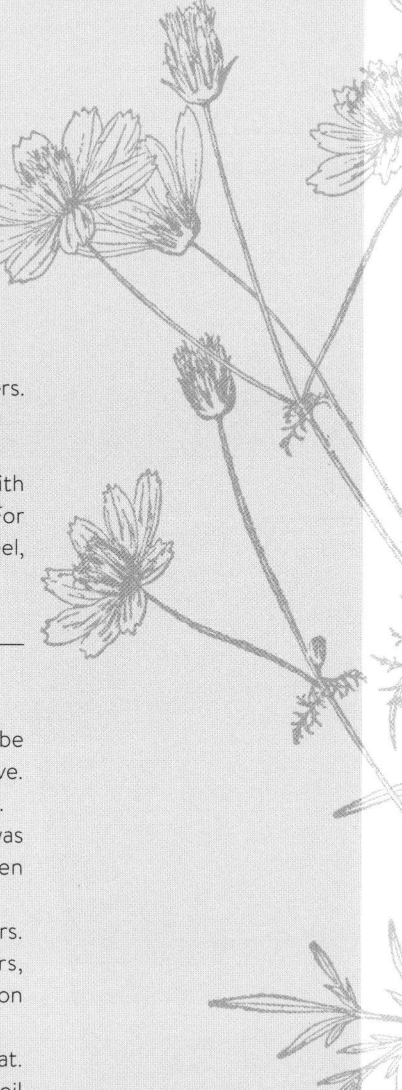

- **Part of plant:** fresh or dried flowers.
- **Harvesting period:** summer.
- **Recommended quantity:** 100–150% of the weight of fiber to be dyed for dried flowers. 200–400% for fresh flowers.
- **Color range:** red, orange.
- **Type of fibers to be dyed and mordant:** suitable for wool. When mordanted with symplocos and a good quantity of plants, cosmos can produce beautiful reds. For plant fibers, galling with colored tannins, such as catechu, chestnut, or onion peel, can produce stronger colors. In all cases, mordanting is necessary.

- Sulfur cosmos is an annual plant in the Asteraceae family, native to Mexico. It can be found all over the United States and Brazil, where locally it is considered as invasive.
- In Indonesia and Thailand, young cosmos plants are eaten raw or cooked in salads.
- Its use as a dye plant goes back to ancient times. A source of oranges and reds, it was used by dyers in pre-Columbian civilizations to dye wool, which had first been mordanted in a decoction of local plants rich in organic aluminum.
- Today, sulfur cosmos is planted in our gardens, on roundabouts, and in urban planters. In addition to its "decorative" aspect, it is particularly popular with pollinators, and just as attractive to you for making beautiful red-oranges! All the more reason to sow it.
- Sow in late spring, in a nursery or in the ground, when frosts are no longer a threat. Sulfur cosmoses like sun and warmth. They are not overly demanding in terms of soil type, provided it has good drainage. In periods of drought, infrequent and abundant watering is necessary. Picking the flowers as you go encourages and prolongs flowering. This means you can pick flowers throughout the summer and dry them for a later dyeing project.
- If you dry them under a press, you can then use the printed flower to make floral designs. But that's another subject.

RECIPE

First step: decoction

1. Put the flowers in a saucepan. Cover with water to immerse the plant and leave to macerate overnight.
2. Gradually raise the temperature to a simmer (185°F/85°C). Maintain this temperature for 30 to 60 minutes. The flowers will lose their color and the liquid will turn red. If the water is acidic, add a little washing soda for a pH of 7 or 8.
3. Turn off the heat. Allow to cool, then strain the decoction through cheesecloth.

Second step: dyeing

1. Pour the plant liquid into a stockpot large enough to allow the fibers to be dyed to spread out.
2. Add enough water to obtain a ratio of approximately 1:20 (see Water, p. 26).
3. Add the mordanted fibers (presoaked and wrung out). Make sure they are completely immersed in the bath.
4. Turn on the heat and gradually raise the temperature to 185°F (85°C). Maintain this temperature for 20 to 60 minutes. Stir regularly (about every 10 minutes) and gently. Turn off the heat and allow the dye bath to cool.

   For silk, the dye bath can be made in cold or even lukewarm water, leaving the fibers to soak for twelve hours and stirring regularly.
5. Once the bath has cooled, remove the fibers and wring them out to dry. Dry out of direct sunlight. Finally, wash with the usual precautions (see Washing, p. 58).

Tansy

Tanacetum vulgare

- **Part of plant:** flowering tops.
- **Harvesting period:** late summer.
- **Recommended quantity:** 500% fresh plants relative to the weight of fiber to be dyed.
- **Color range:** shades of yellow, tawny brown, gray.
- **Type of fibers to be dyed and mordant:** works on all fibers, with any type of plant mordant. If you are looking for a deep yellow, wool mordanted with symplocos or green tea is best.

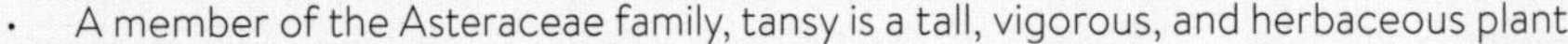

- A member of the Asteraceae family, tansy is a tall, vigorous, and herbaceous plant.
- Well-known in the Middle Ages, it was listed as a medicinal plant and grown in every garden. Because of its slightly spicy aroma, it was used as a seasoning to replace cinnamon or nutmeg, which were very expensive at the time.
- However, due to its high concentration of thujone, a potentially toxic chemical compound, its medicinal use has been abandoned.
- On the other hand, tansy is a precious ally in the garden. Thanks to its insect-repellent, fungicidal, and pest-repellent properties, it has a natural place in orchards, at the foot of peach and pear trees. Some use it in the form of a fertilizer to protect certain crops.
- At home, you can make moth-proof sachets or bouquets out of tansy to protect your woolen goods.
- This large perennial with a rather exuberant temperament is easy to grow. If you would like to plant it at home, in March, pick a small clump of suckering buds from a friendly garden. Transplant it to a wild corner of your garden, where you do not have to worry about it spreading out. Perched on its tall stems, it can sometimes have a hard time staying up. Give it a hand with stakes.
- When it starts to flower, its buds are bright yellow, darkening as the season progresses. The time you harvest the flowers will influence the shades of yellow. Fresh flowers are preferred for brighter shades.
- Tansy is rich in flavonoids and tannins.

RECIPE

First step: decoction

1. Put the flower buds in a saucepan. Leave overnight.
2. Turn on the heat and gradually raise the temperature to a simmer (185–195°F/85–90°C). Maintain this temperature for 15 minutes. Check the pH of the decoction, adding washing soda if necessary to bring the pH to 8. The liquid will turn yellow-orange.
3. Turn off the heat. Cool and strain through cheesecloth. Reserve the liquid.

Second step: dyeing

1. Pour the plant liquid into a stockpot large enough to allow the fibers to be dyed to spread out.
2. Add water to obtain a ratio of approximately 1:20 (see Water, p. 26). Check the pH of the bath and add a little washing soda if necessary, for a pH of 8.
3. Add the mordanted fibers (presoaked and wrung out). Make sure they are completely immersed in the bath.
4. Turn on the heat and gradually increase the temperature to around 185°F (85°C). Maintain this temperature for 15 minutes. Avoid simmering any longer than this. As tansy is rich in tannins, too long a boil may dull the color somewhat.

   Stir regularly (approximately every 10 minutes) and gently. Turn off the heat and allow the dye bath to cool.

   For silk, the dye bath can be made in cold or even lukewarm water, leaving the fibers to soak for 12 hours and stirring regularly.
5. Once the bath has cooled, remove the fibers and wring out to dry. Dry away from direct sunlight. Finally, wash with the usual precautions (see Washing, p. 58).

For plant fibers, passing through iron liquid will make the color greener.

Weld

Dyer's rocket, dyer's weed, or yellow weed

Reseda luteola

- **Part of plant:** aerial part.
- **Harvesting period:** late summer or early autumn, when it goes to seed.
- **Recommended quantity:** 100% of the weight of fiber to be dyed for a dry plant. 200–300% for a fresh plant.
- **Color range:** yellow.
- **Type of fibers to be dyed and mordant:** works on all fibers. However, the most beautiful yellows are obtained with wool and silk, in the form of tangy, luminous yellows. Mordanting is necessary. Luteolin, the plant's main yellow colorant, needs the aluminum ion to bind to fibers. So use a plant rich in organic aluminum, such as symplocos, for mordanting.

- Weld has a prestigious past as a dye plant. In the Middle Ages and Renaissance, it was the yellow plant: bright, vivid and, most importantly, long-lasting. It was widely cultivated for this purpose, particularly in the Mediterranean basin.
- The arrival of synthetic dyes in the nineteenth century and the manufacture of cotton fabrics made weld less attractive. Gradually, its cultivation and dyeing uses were abandoned.
- If you take a walk in a dry, sunny wasteland with volcanic or limestone soil, you may be able to spot it in the wild. It is a biennial plant, known as a "ruderal": it grows spontaneously on soil that has recently been disturbed and enriched with nutrients. This is often land that has been worked on or even disturbed by people. It colonizes vacant lots, wastelands, freeway embankments, and piles of backfill. Its tall stems and tiny yellow flowers are hard to miss.
- Nevertheless, it is still possible to grow it in the garden, if your soil is suited to its needs. Like all biennial plants, it is sown in autumn and will form a small rosette over winter. The following spring, it develops a large, more or less branched flowering spike, with small yellow flowers at the tip. It can be harvested as soon as it sets seed and the base leaves turn yellow. It can be used fresh, after you have collected a few seeds for reseeding. If you can, be sure to keep the seed husks, which are rich in colorant. The plant can also be dried and ground.

RECIPE

First step: decoction

1 Put the crushed plant in a saucepan. Cover with water, preferably hard water. If using soft water, add a pinch of chalk (calcium carbonate). Leave to stand overnight.

2 Turn on the heat, gradually raising the temperature to a simmer (185–195°F/85–90°C). Maintain this temperature for 20 to 60 minutes, depending on the quantity of plant material.

3 Turn off the heat. Cool and strain the decoction through cheesecloth. Reserve the liquid.

Second step: dyeing

1 Pour the plant liquid into a stockpot large enough to allow the fibers to be dyed to spread out.

2 Add water, hard water if possible, to obtain a ratio of approximately 1:20 (see Water, p. 26).

If the water used is soft, like mine, add 1 teaspoon of chalk for every 2.5 gallons (10 liters) of water.

Check the pH of the bath and add a little washing soda if necessary for a pH of 7 or 8.

3 Add the mordanted fibers (presoaked and wrung out). Make sure they are completely immersed in the bath.

4 Heat and very gradually raise the temperature to a simmer (185–195°F/85–90°C). Maintain at this temperature for 20 to 60 minutes.

Stir regularly (approximately every 10 minutes) and gently. Turn off the heat and allow the dye bath to cool.

For silk, the dye bath can be made in cold or even lukewarm water, leaving the fibers to soak for 12 hours and stirring regularly.

5 Once the bath has cooled, remove the fibers and wring out to dry. Dry away from direct sunlight. Finally, wash with the usual precautions (see Washing, p. 58). However, if, as in my case, the water used is very soft and slightly acidic, washing with a little dish soap or chalk will intensify the yellow.

Rudbeckia

Rudbeckia fulgida

- **Part of plant:** whole plant.
- **Harvesting period:** summer.
- **Recommended quantity:** 600–800% fresh plant relative to the weight of fiber to be dyed.
- **Color range:** shades of pink, green, yellow.
- **Type of fibers to be dyed and mordant:** suitable for all fibers, animal or vegetable, with any type of vegetable mordant.

- If there is one flower in the garden that knows how to make a statement, it is the black-eyed Susan. With its stiff stems pointing toward the sun and the yellow-orange of its petals surrounding a domed crimson-brown heart, it shows a certain self-confidence.
- A member of the Asteraceae family and native to the United States and Mexico, it is an undemanding perennial that thrives in even the poorest soils. It tolerates drought relatively well and will flourish if it can take advantage of the sun. If it is doing well, it will spread readily.
- You can pick it all summer long. Not intended for drying, rudbeckia can be used as a fresh dye. For strong colors, a heavy weight of plant is recommended. This is relatively easy to obtain, as the flowers are heavy.
- The plant is picked whole. You then separate the flowers from the stems and leaves, to make two different dyes: yellows and greens with the stems and leaves cut small, and purplish pinks with the flowers left whole.
- This is an interesting dyeing experiment: one plant for two different shades of color, depending on the part being used. This color variability is explained by the diversity of its chemical components, all of which belong to the flavonoid family of yellows. However, a high concentration of anthocyanins in the flowers explains the shades of pink.

RECIPE

First step: decoction

1 Make two pots: one for the flowers, the other for the stems and leaves. Cover with water and leave to stand for a few hours.
2 Adjust the pH of each decoction: for the flowers, add lemon juice for a pH of 4; for the stems and leaves, the pH should be 7 or 8. Add washing soda if necessary. Turn on the heat and gradually raise the temperature to just below 175°F (80°C). Maintain this temperature for 1 hour, or a little longer for large quantities of plant. The flower liquid will turn red, while the leaf and stem juice will gradually turn greenish-yellow.
3 Turn off the heat. Allow to cool and strain the decoctions through cheesecloth.
4 Leave the juices to mature overnight.

Second step: dyeing

1 Pour the plant liquids into two stockpots large enough to allow the fibers to be dyed to spread out.
2 Add water to obtain a ratio of approximately 1:20 (see Water, p. 26).

   Check the pH of the baths: pH 4 of flowers and pH of 7 or 8 for stems and leaves. If necessary, add lemon juice or washing soda.
3 Dip the mordanted fibers (presoaked and wrung out) into the bath. Make sure they are completely immersed in the bath.
4 Heat to just below the simmering point (175°F/80°C). Do not boil. Maintain this temperature for at least 1 hour.

   Stir regularly (approximately every 10 minutes) and gently. Turn off the heat and allow the dye baths to cool.

   For silk, the dye bath can be made in cold or even lukewarm water, leaving the fibers to soak for 12 hours and stirring regularly.
5 Once the baths have cooled, remove the fibers and wring out to dry. Dry away from direct sunlight. Finally, wash with the usual precautions (see Washing, p. 58).

Buckwheat

Fagopyrum esculentum

- **Part of plant:** aerial part of flower.
- **Harvesting period:** summer.
- **Recommended quantity:** 400% of fresh plant relative to the weight of fiber to be dyed.
- **Color range:** orange-yellow, pinkish-beige, khaki green.
- **Type of fibers to be dyed and mordant:** this plant has a better affinity with wool and silk and can be dyed with any type of vegetable mordant. On animal fibers, the tones will tend toward yellow-orange.

- Buckwheat is an annual plant that I am particularly fond of. With a preference for poor, slightly acidic soils, buckwheat does particularly well where I live. I sow it in late spring, as soon as there is no longer any risk of frost, in slightly empty corners of the garden. In its early stages of growth, it needs warmth and humidity. Regular watering may be necessary.
- Fast-growing, it produces beautiful beds of small, pinkish-white flowers, perched high on slender stems, clothed in beautiful heart-shaped leaves.
- It is a charming plant that provides many services in the garden. It is particularly melliferous, and buckwheat honey has a unique taste. It is classified as a companion plant and is used as a green fertilizer. Its ability to take over spontaneous, self-propagating plants makes it an invaluable ally for covering slightly bare soil. Combined with phacelia, it creates beautiful, wild-looking flowerbeds that foraging insects will appreciate.
- If you sow it in large quantities, you can try your hand at making your own flour or dye.
- Buckwheat should be picked during the summer, when it is in full bloom, or just as it is coming to the end of its blooming season. The colors are brighter if the decoction is made from fresh plants.
- If you do not have the opportunity to sow buckwheat, you can approach a grower and ask if they will allow you to pick up a few armfuls of the plant.

RECIPE

First step: decoction

1. Put the flowering buckwheat stalks, cut into small sections, in a saucepan. Cover with water to immerse the plant.
2. Gradually heat to a simmer (185–195°F/85–90°C). Maintain this temperature for 30 to 60 minutes, depending on the quantity of plant material used. If the water used is acidic, add a little washing soda for a pH of 7 or 8.
3. Turn off the heat. Cool and strain the decoction through cheesecloth. Reserve the dye liquid.

Second step: dyeing

1. Pour the dye liquid into a stockpot large enough to allow the fibers to be dyed to spread out.
2. Add water to obtain a ratio of approximately 1:20 (see Water, p. 26). Check the bath pH. If necessary, add a pinch of washing soda for a pH of 7 or 8.
3. Add the mordanted fibers (presoaked and wrung out). Make sure they are completely immersed in the bath.
4. Heat and gradually raise the temperature to 185°F (85°C), maintaining it for 20 to 60 minutes. Stir regularly (every 10 minutes or so) and gently. Turn off the heat and allow the dye bath to cool.

   For silk, the dye bath can be made in cold or even lukewarm water, leaving the fibers to soak for 12 hours and stirring regularly.
5. Once the bath has cooled, remove the fibers and wring out to dry. Dry away from direct sunlight. Finally, wash with the usual precautions (see Washing, p. 58).

   Plant fibers treated with iron water will turn khaki green.

Madder

Dyer's madder

Rubia tinctorum

- **Part of plant:** small or crushed cut roots.
- **Harvesting period:** autumn, from plants at least three years old.
- **Recommended quantity:** 100% of the weight of fiber to be dyed.
- **Color range:** red, orange, pink, violet.
- **Type of fibers to be dyed and mordant:** intense reds are more easily obtained on wool. On vegetable fibers, pink and pinkish shades are easily obtained. If you are looking for a "true" red, choose a wool with symplocos mordant. If you want a deep red on plant fibers, you'll need to alternate between mordant baths and symplocos (see Mordant using symplocos, p. 46).

- If you grow madder in the garden, wait three years before harvesting. This is a prerequisite for larger, longer roots and, consequently, higher yields. Pulling out the roots is not always easy. Once harvested, wash and dry them for a few months before cutting them into small sections.
- If you do not grow madder, but happen to travel to the Mediterranean region, you may come across its cousin, wild madder (*Rubia peregrina*), at the foot of a hedge or embankment. It differs from dyer's madder in its evergreen foliage and also in the composition of its rhizomes. Containing little alizarin, they are rich in other colorants, all belonging to the red family, and offer reds in more brick-like shades.
- In my garden, I have bedstraw, which grows in slightly acidic, loamy soil. They, too, belong to the Rubiaceae family of red plants. However, the fineness of their roots makes harvesting them tricky and the work of peeling them very tedious (see photo opposite of bedstraw roots).
- Another member of the Rubiaceae family that I particularly like is Indian madder (*Rubia cordifolia*).
- If you buy madder, the quality varies from one supplier to another. In fact, even with the same supplier, shades can change from one year to the next. The nature of the soil, the harvesting period, and the climate are all factors that influence the concentration of colorants.

RECIPE

First step: decoction

1. Put madder roots in a saucepan. Cover with water to immerse the plant. Leave to stand overnight, or optimally twenty-four hours.
2. Heat slowly to 175°F (80°C). Do not boil.
3. Turn off the heat. Cool and strain the decoction through cheesecloth. Reserve the dye liquid.

   For a higher concentration of colorant, you can repeat and make a second decoction with the plant material recovered through the cheesecloth. Add the second dye liquid to the first.

Second step: dyeing

1. Pour the dye liquid into a stockpot large enough to allow the fibers to be dyed to spread out.
2. Add water, hard water if possible, to obtain a ratio of approximately 1:20 (see Water, p. 26).

   If the water used is soft, like mine, add 1 teaspoon of chalk for every 2.5 gallons (10 liters) of water. This is a guideline that does not necessarily have to be followed to the letter. Remember, madder likes alkaline, carbonate-rich soil. Hard water with a pH of around 8 allows madder to express its best qualities. Keep an eye on the color of the bath: the redder, the better.
3. Add the mordanted fibers (presoaked and wrung out). Make sure they are completely immersed in the bath.
4. Heat and gradually raise the temperature to 175°F (80°C). Maintain this temperature for 20 to 60 minutes.

   Do not heat to boiling point, as this will alter the color, turning the red to brown.

   Stir regularly (approximately every 10 minutes) and gently. Turn off the heat and allow the dye bath to cool.

   For silk, you can make the dye bath cold, leaving the fibers to soak for 12 hours and stirring regularly.
5. Once the bath has cooled, remove the fibers and wring out dry. Dry away from direct sunlight. Finally, wash with the usual precautions (see Washing, p. 58). If, as in my case, the water used is not very hard and slightly acidic, washing with a little dish soap or chalk will slightly redden the shades.

   Plant fibers will take on shades of violet or brick red when passed through iron water.

   Once your dyeing is finished, the madder is not exhausted. The power of its dyes means you can obtain pretty oranges and pinks with a second dye bath.

IN THE KITCHEN: VEGETABLE PLANTS

The first color resource, accessible to all, is found in your kitchen and vegetable garden, if you have one.

The advantage is that you can make color out of the vegetable scraps you have used for cooking. It is a different way to recycle organic waste.

For some of these plants, the dyeing process is very simple, since the preliminary step of mordanting is unnecessary or optional.

Avocado

Persea americana

- **Part of plant:** fruit skins and pits.
- **Harvesting period:** autumn and winter.
- **Recommended quantity:** 100–200% of the weight of fibers to be dyed for dry skins. 50–100% for pits.
- **Color range:** shades of salmon, pink, violet.
- **Type of fibers to be dyed and mordant:** suitable for all fibers. No mordanting required. Plant fibers offer very pretty shades of pink.

- The avocado is the fruit of the avocado tree, a member of the Lauraceae family native to Mexico and Central America. This evergreen tree, which can grow from eight to twenty meters high, blooms abundantly in summer. Only 1 percent of its flowers will bear fruit. Its natural habitat is the tropical forest, so it needs warmth and humidity. It thrives in light, well-drained, neutral or acidic humus-bearing soils. It does not tolerate frost or drought.
- In the sixteenth century, it was imported to Spain, where it was first cultivated for its ornamental qualities, before the alimentary qualities of its fruit were discovered. In France, production began in the 1950s, particularly in Corsica. Today, there is a real craze for avocados. It has become a staple food, and its nutritional qualities are rightly praised. But the other side of the coin is sad. To satisfy ever-increasing demand, producing countries are subjected to massive deforestation and drying up of their water tables, all with a heavy carbon footprint linked to the conditions under which the imported fruit is transported, preserved, and stored.
- In these conditions, making color by recycling avocado waste is an eco-friendly approach, as long as the fruit is consumed in moderation, in season, and using the shortest possible supply channels.
- Once the fruit has been consumed, it is important to dry the skins and pits properly to avoid any mold. After scraping off the remaining flesh, you can quickly run them under water before drying them near a heat source.
- Once dried, the skins can be easily crushed. The pits, on the other hand, are more difficult. You can help yourself to a hammer.
- You can use skins and pits in the same bath for redder tones, or use them separately. The pits alone offer flesh tones, while the skins have more orange or red tones, depending on the pH of the bath.

RECIPE

First step: decoction

1 Put the crushed skins and pits in a saucepan. Cover with water. If the water used is slightly chalky and basic (pH around 8), the tones will tend toward pink, red, and brown. With more acidic or soft water (pH around 6), the tones will be more orangey or salmon.
2 Turn on the heat and gradually raise the temperature to a simmer (185–195°F/85–90°C). Adjust the pH of the decoction according to the desired shade: more alkaline with washing soda for a pH of around 8, or more acidic with lemon juice for a pH of around 6. Keep at low boil for 30 to 60 minutes, depending on the quantity of plant material. Add water if evaporation occurs in order to keep the plant submerged.
3 Turn off the heat. Cool and strain the decoction through cheesecloth. Reserve the dye liquid.

For a higher concentration of colorant, you can repeat and make a second decoction with the plant material recovered through the cheesecloth. Add the second dye liquid to the first.

Leave the resulting liquid to stand for 12 to 24 hours. Maturation of the juice results in more uniform colors.

Second step: dyeing

1 Pour the dye liquid into a stockpot large enough to allow the fibers to be dyed to spread out.
2 Add water to obtain a ratio of approximately 1:20 (see Water, p. 26). Check the pH of the bath and adjust its level according to the shade desired, as previously indicated.
3 Add the fibers (presoaked and wrung out). Make sure they are completely immersed in the bath.
4 Turn on the heat and gradually raise the temperature to a simmer (185–195°F/85–90°C). Keep at this temperature for about 1 hour. Stir regularly (about every 10 minutes) and gently. To avoid oxidation, make sure the fibers are completely immersed throughout cooking, otherwise marbling may occur. Turn off the heat and allow the dye bath to cool.

For silk, the dye bath can be made in cold or even lukewarm water, leaving the fibers to soak for 12 hours and stirring regularly.
5 Once the bath has cooled, remove the fibers and wring out dry. Dry away from direct sunlight. Finally, wash with the usual precautions (see Washing, p. 58), although avocado color is reputed to be resistant to washing and light.

When passed through iron water, the plant fibers will take on beautiful shades of violet or lilac blue.

Onion

Allium cepa

- **Part of plant:** outer peel.
- **Harvesting period:** year-round from your local store or organic market or from April to August in the vegetable garden.
- **Recommended quantity:** at least 100% of the weight of fiber to be dyed.
- **Color range:** yellow, orange, pink, pinkish-brown, tan, plum, green.
- **Type of fibers to be dyed and mordant:** shades vary considerably according to the nature of the fibers: yellow and orange for animal fibers and pink, brown, and tan for plant fibers. Mordanting is optional. It does, however, produce more intense, longer-lasting colors. All mordant plants are suitable.

- Onion peels are easy to harvest, the best place being the bottom of the crates where onions are stored. Of course, I recommend that you choose organically grown onions. You can then collect this vegetable waste in large quantities year-round and store them in a brown paper bag or crate, in a dry place.
- Be sure to keep only the dry outer skins, which are richer in colorant, allowing you to avoid mold.
- Red and yellow onions work equally well. They offer different shades of color. Do not hesitate to mix them to broaden the color palette.
- Onion peels are rich in quercetin, a yellow colorant from the flavonoid family. Red onions are among the plants richest in quercetin.
- In addition to offering magnificent shades, quercetin is known in herbal medicine for its anti-inflammatory, antihistaminic, and invigorating properties on the body.

RECIPE

First step: decoction

1 Put the peels in a saucepan. Cover with water to immerse the plant. Leave overnight.

2 Bring to a simmer (185°F/85°C). During cooking, add washing soda for a pH of 8. The liquid will turn red. Maintain this temperature for 45 to 90 minutes, depending on the quantity of plant material. Add water if evaporation occurs, in order to keep the plant fully submerged.

3 Turn off the heat. Cool and strain the decoction through cheesecloth. Reserve the dye liquid.

For a higher concentration of colorant, you can repeat and make a second decoction with the plant material recovered through the cheesecloth. Add the second dye liquid to the first.

Leave the resulting liquid to stand overnight.

Second step: dyeing

1 Pour the dye liquid into a stockpot large enough to allow the fibers to be dyed to spread out.

2 Add water to obtain a ratio of approximately 1:20 (see Water, p. 26). Check the bath pH (it should be between 7 and 8). Add washing soda if necessary.

3 Add the fibers, mordanted or not (presoaked and wrung out). Make sure they are completely immersed in the bath.

4 Turn on the heat and gradually raise the temperature to a simmer (185°F/85°C). Simmer for about 1 hour, adding hot water to keep the fibers submerged.

Stir regularly (approximately every 10 minutes) and gently. Turn off the heat and allow the dye bath to cool.

For silk, you can make the dye bath cold, leaving the fibers to soak for 12 hours and stirring regularly.

5 Once the bath has cooled, remove the fibers and wring out to dry. Dry away from direct sunlight. Finally, wash with the usual precautions (see Washing, p. 58). For onions, washing with an eco-friendly soap-based detergent is not a problem. Onions like alkaline environments, which allow them to express their most beautiful tawny hues.

Plant fibers dyed with iron water will take on beautiful shades of bottle green or khaki green. On fibers previously dyed indigo, you'll obtain dark greens.

Turmeric

Curcuma longa

- **Part of plant:** rhizome.
- **Harvesting period:** year-round from your organic grocer.
- **Recommended quantity:** at least 100% of the weight of fibers to be dyed.
- **Color range:** shades of yellow (bright yellow, orange yellow, mustard yellow), brick red, reddish-brown.
- **Type of fibers to be dyed and mordant:** all types of fiber, animal or plant. No mordanting required.

- Turmeric is a herbaceous plant, growing no more than three feet high, with many perennial rhizomes. It is native to India, which remains the world's leading producer of it. A plant of tropical climates, it needs rich, well-drained soil, as well as warmth and humidity.
- The rhizomes are rich in curcuminoids, the chemical compounds responsible for the plant's yellow-orange color. Their content varies according to climate and variety.
- A plant steeped in history and symbolism, turmeric is certainly one of the best-known spices. Consumed mainly in the form of curry, it is an essential ingredient in Indian cuisine, with its distinctive flavor and color.
- The use of turmeric in herbal medicine has been the subject of much research: its anti-inflammatory, hepatoprotective, and neuroprotective properties, as well as its anticancer potential, make it a major medicinal plant.
- Last but not least, its use as a dye plant goes back a long way. It is widespread in India and throughout Southeast Asia. Everyone knows the orangey-yellow robes worn by Buddhist monks. In Europe, during the centuries of plant-based dyes, the plant was little used: it was only used to enhance the yellow of a rather bland weld.
- Good to eat, useful for healing, and effective for coloring dishes, skins, and textiles—that is a lot of qualities for one plant. It does, however, have one weakness: the color it generously offers is fragile and tends to fade in the sun.

RECIPE

First step: decoction

1 Place the turmeric rhizome in a saucepan. Cover with water to immerse the plant.
2 Turn on the heat and gradually raise the temperature to a simmer (195°F/90°C). Stir regularly, being careful not to let the water splash. Maintain this temperature for 20 to 30 minutes, depending on the quantity of plant material used. Add water if evaporation occurs in order to keep the plant material submerged.
3 Turn off the heat. Cool and strain the decoction through cheesecloth. Reserve the dye liquid after adding lemon juice.

Second step: dyeing

1 Pour the dye liquid into a stockpot large enough to allow the fibers to be dyed to spread out.
2 Add water to obtain a ratio of approximately 1:20 (see Water, p. 26). Add lemon juice for a pH between 4 and 5.
3 Add presoaked, wrung-out fibers. Make sure they are completely immersed in the bath.
4 Heat and gradually raise the temperature to boiling (185–195°F/85–90°C). Boil for about 1 hour, adding hot water to keep fibers submerged.

Stir regularly (approximately every 10 minutes) and gently. Turn off the heat and allow the dye bath to cool.

For silk, you can make the dye bath cold, leaving the fibers to soak for 12 hours, stirring regularly.

5 Once the bath has cooled, remove the fibers and wring dry. Dry out of direct sunlight. Finally, wash with the usual precautions (see Washing, p. 58).

Turmeric's bright yellow color does not stand up well to light. In full sun, the yellow fades. It is therefore a color to be reserved for indoor fabrics. There's nothing to stop you redyeing when you feel the yellow has lost its brightness.

I've found that turmeric treated with iron water stands up better to the sun. In this case, the shades of yellow will turn tawny, mustard, or even khaki, depending on the variety of curcuma. Iron water only works on plant fibers.

Similarly, on plant fibers, you can change the color to a reddish-brown by soaking the fabric for a few minutes in hot water with washing soda (pH of 8 to 9).

Beet

Beta vulgaris

- **Part of plant:** lacto-fermented root juice.
- **Harvesting period:** early summer to autumn.
- **Recommended quantity:** at least 100% of the weight of fiber to be dyed.
- **Color range:** violet, burgundy red, orange-yellow.
- **Type of fibers to be dyed and mordant:** animal fibers only (wool and silk). Mordanting is not necessary; I found no difference in shade in a comparative test with and without mordant.

- This recipe was inspired by a friend of mine who is a lacto-fermentation cook. One day, she brought me some jars of lacto-fermented beet juice and asked me about the color: she had read on the Internet that lacto-fermented beet juice gave a long-lasting yellow color, but had no further details.
- Beet roots are very rich in betalains, which are very bright colorants. However, these dyes have a well-deserved reputation for being very fragile and not very long-lasting on textile fibers. So there was a mystery to be unraveled, which aroused my curiosity.
- Without delay, I set to work on my pots. To my astonishment, I found that lacto-fermented beet juice could be used to obtain shades of pink-purple, red, and yellow-orange, without the need for prior mordanting. I noticed that the different shades obtained depended on the concentration of betalains in the juice, as well as on the temperature and duration of cooking. The colors held up perfectly to washing. Some shades faded a little after several months of UV exposure behind a window.
- All this is empirical, and only for those who like to experiment and recycle. If you like beets and are a fan of lacto-fermentation, then know that you can make color instead of discarding your juice.
- This experiment illustrates that lacto-fermentation is more than just a preservation method: the plant is truly transformed. Thanks to the work of the bacteria, the color goes from fleeting to long-lasting.

RECIPE

Lacto-fermented beet juice

For a 4-cup (approx. 1-liter) jar: 2 lb (approx. 1 kg) beets, unchlorinated water, and unrefined salt.

1 Dice beets without peeling them.
2 Dissolve 2 teaspoons (10 g) of salt in 4 cups (1 liter) of water. This is the brine.
3 Fill the jar with the diced beets and pour the brine over it to within 1 inch (2 centimeters) of the rim. Make sure the beets are completely submerged.
4 Seal the jar tightly with a jar seal. Leave to mature in a cool place (60–65°F/16–18°C) at a constant temperature, for at least 6 months.

  The longer the ripening time, the more concentrated your juice will be in betalains. After eating the beets, save the juice for dyeing.

Dye

1 Pour the juice into a stockpot large enough to allow the fibers to be dyed to adequately spread out. Turn on the heat.
2 Add fresh water (preferably rainwater) to obtain a ratio of approximately 1:20 (see Water, p. 26).
3 Add presoaked, wrung-out fibers. Make sure they are completely immersed in the bath.
4 Gradually raise the temperature, stirring regularly. Below the simmering point (175°F/80°C), shades tend to be pinkish-purple. Above the simmering point, shades will turn red.

  Stir regularly (approximately every 10 minutes) and gently.
5 Turn off heat when desired color appears. Let cool before removing fibers. A second bath will produce more yellow- orange colors.

Carrot

Daucus carota subsp. *sativus*

- **Part of plant:** fresh leaves.
- **Harvesting period:** from spring to autumn in the vegetable garden or at your organic farmers markets.
- **Recommended quantity:** at least 400% of the weight of fiber to be dyed.
- **Color range:** shades of yellow.
- **Type of fibers to be dyed and mordant:** animal fibers (wool or silk) with beet leaf mordant.

- Cooking vegetable tops to create a fully plant-based color struck me one day at the market, as I looked at the crates from the organic farmers market filled with carrot and beet tops destined for chickens or compost. I asked to take some.
- Once back home and after quickly weighing my harvest, I put carrot and beet tops into a pot and heated them together. The idea was not to make the most beautiful yellow, but to create, in a simple way, color solely from vegetable tops.
- Unlike avocado skin or onion peel, which are usable plants without prior mordanting, carrot tops need a mordant. To do this, beet tops work very well. However, you can experiment with a mordant plant of your choice.
- Let your decoction mature for a few days; the result will be better.

RECIPE

First step: decoction

1. Place the finely chopped carrot tops in a saucepan. Cover with water to immerse the plant. Leave to stand overnight.
2. Bring to a simmer (195°F/90°C). While simmering, add washing soda for a pH of 8. Keep at this temperature for 45 to 90 minutes, depending on the quantity of plant material. Add water if evaporation occurs in order to keep the plant submerged.
3. Turn off the heat. Cool and strain the decoction through cheesecloth. Reserve the dye liquid.

   Leave the liquid to stand overnight.

Second step: dyeing

1. Pour the dye liquid into a stockpot large enough to allow the fibers to be dyed to spread out.
2. Add water to obtain a ratio of approximately 1:20 (see Water, p. 26). Check the bath pH (it should be between 7 and 8). Add washing soda if necessary.
3. Add the mordanted fibers (presoaked and wrung out). Make sure they are completely immersed in the bath.
4. Turn on the heat and gradually increase the temperature to a boiling point (185–195°F/85–90°C). Boil for about 1 hour, adding hot water to keep the fibers submerged.

   Stir regularly (approximately every 10 minutes) and gently. Turn off the heat and allow the dye bath to cool.

   For silk, you can make the dye bath cold, leaving the fibers to soak for 12 hours and stirring regularly.
5. Once the bath has cooled, remove the fibers and wring them out dry. Dry out of direct sunlight. Then wash with the usual precautions (see Washing, p. 58).

Rhubarb

Rheum species

- **Part of plant:** fresh or dried roots ground into powder.
- **Harvesting period:** summer. If you do not grow rhubarb, you can obtain it in extract form from a herbalist or stores specializing in plant dyes.
- **Recommended quantity:** 100% of the weight of fibers to be dyed for a dried plant. 200% for a fresh plant.
- **Color range:** shades of yellow, yellow orange.
- **Type of fibers to be dyed and mordant:** best affinity with animal fibers (wool or silk). All types of mordant.

- Rhubarb is a perennial herbaceous plant in the Polygonaceae family. There are many varieties, such as Chinese rhubarb, Indian rhubarb, and rhapontic rhubarb.
- Native to northwestern China and Tibet, where it grows wild, rhubarb can grow up to six feet tall, with large, well-lobed leaves.
- Hybrid varieties of rhubarb that are adapted to temperate climates can be grown in the garden for the pleasure of cooking it in the form of pie or jam. However, with climate change and increasingly long periods of drought, garden rhubarb is finding it hard to flourish in summer. It thrives in sunny, deep, fertile, well-drained soil that stays cool in summer.
- A medicinal plant in traditional Chinese medicine, it is mainly known for its tonic and purgative properties.
- Its use as a dye plant goes back a long way. Like weld for eighteenth-century Europeans, rhubarb is the Tibetans' main source of yellow and orange, as evidenced by their magnificent carpets.
- I'm particularly fond of using rhubarb in dyeing, for its shades of golden yellow to mustard yellow, or orange when mordanted with beet leaves.
- It is a multipurpose plant for the dyer: its oxalic acid–rich leaves (see Plants rich in oxalic acid, p. 37) can be used as a mordant, and its roots as a coloring agent.
- The concentration of anthraquinone derivatives, responsible for the yellow color, varies from one rhubarb variety to another. This explains the differences in hue between plants, as well as between seasons.

RECIPE

First step: decoction

1 Place the powdered or finely chopped roots in a saucepan. Cover with water to ensure immersion.
2 Turn on the heat and gradually raise the temperature to a simmer (185°F/85°C). Stir regularly. Maintain this temperature for 30 to 60 minutes, depending on the quantity of plant material used. Add water if evaporation occurs in order to keep the plant submerged.
3 Turn off the heat. Cool and strain the decoction through cheesecloth. Reserve the dye liquid after adding lemon juice for a pH between 4 and 6.

For a higher concentration of colorant, you can repeat this step and make a second decoction with the plant material recovered from the cheesecloth. Add the second dye liquid to the first.

Second step: dyeing

1 Pour the dye liquid into a stockpot large enough to allow the fibers to be dyed to spread out.
2 Add water to obtain a ratio of approximately 1:20 (see Water, p. 26). Check the bath pH (it should be between 4 and 6). Add lemon juice if necessary.
3 Add the mordanted fibers (presoaked and wrung out). Make sure they are completely immersed in the dye bath.
4 Turn on the heat and gradually raise the temperature to a simmer (185–195°F/85–90°C). Simmer for 30 to 60 minutes, adding hot water to keep the fibers submerged.

Stir regularly (approximately every 10 minutes) and gently. Turn off the heat and allow the dye bath to cool.

For silk, you can make the dye bath cold, leaving the fibers to soak for 12 hours and stirring regularly.

5 Once the bath has cooled, remove the fibers and wring out to dry. Dry out of direct sunlight. Finally, wash with the usual precautions (see Washing, p. 58).

Rhubarb yellow is lightfast and washable. In slightly acidic water, it will retain its brilliance.

Beautiful greens can be obtained on wool dyed with indigo, and luminous oranges on wool mordanted with beetroot.

ALONG THE PATHS: WILD PLANTS

The banks and ditches of country paths, like road embankments, are often ideal habitats for biodiversity. Uncultivated and untreated, wild plants flourish, providing shelter and food for a whole host of wildlife.

When you are interested in plant color, you take a close look at the diversity of flora that develops according to the nature of the site, whether cool and humid, forested, or dry and arid.

I am going to tell you about the plants I have picked around my home. But, of course, there are many others.

It is a pity that they are still too often considered as weeds. As botanist Gérard Ducerf so aptly put it, "a weed is only a plant whose usefulness is unknown." Plant-based dyeing can help you discover the fabulous resources of these wild plants.

Goldenrod

Solidago species

- **Part of plant:** flowering tops.
- **Harvesting period:** late summer or early autumn, when the plant goes to seed.
- **Recommended quantity:** 100% of the weight of the fibers to be dyed for dry plant. 200–300% for fresh plant.
- **Color range:** yellow.
- **Type of fibers to be dyed and mordant:** works on all fibers. However, the most beautiful yellows are obtained with wool and silk. Mordanting is necessary. For a bright yellow, mordanting with symplocos is recommended.

- Undemanding and hardy, this perennial of the Asteraceae family delights bees in late summer. Goldenrod lights up roadsides and ditches at the end of the season with its golden-yellow flowering stems. Where I live, I'm also lucky enough to come across it at the edge of coniferous forests. It thrives in sunny, fertile, well-drained soil.
- The goldenrod of European roadsides (*Solidago virgaurea*) must be distinguished from the American varieties, *Solidago canadensis* and *Solidago gigantea*, which have an unfortunate tendency to be invasive and harm biodiversity.
- Goldenrod has been recognized as a medicinal plant since the Middle Ages. It was used to heal wounds, hence its name derived from the Latin *solidare*, meaning "to strengthen" the edges of wounds. Today, in herbal medicine, it is a plant of first resort for urinary tract infections. Its richness in flavonoids, particularly quercetin, the chemical compound responsible for its yellow color, gives it antioxidant, antimicrobial, and antifungal properties. It is also used for its detoxifying properties.
- When you are out walking in late summer, keep an eye on the slopes and embankments. Your eye will quickly be drawn to the luminous yellow of goldenrod. You will be able to pick it as it begins to bloom while respecting the usual rules for picking (see Wild foraging: harvesting without harming, p. 25). I recommend using it fresh. When you get home, use a pair of pruning shears to cut it into small pieces.

RECIPE

First step: decoction

1. Put the finely chopped flowers in a saucepan. Cover with water, preferably hard water. If using soft water, add a pinch of chalk (calcium carbonate). Leave to stand overnight.
2. Turn on the heat and gradually raise the temperature to a simmer (185–195°F/85–90°C). Keep at this temperature for 20 to 60 minutes, depending on the quantity of plant material.
3. Turn off the heat. Cool and strain the decoction through cheesecloth. Reserve the dye liquid.

Second step: dyeing

1. Pour the dye liquid into a stockpot large enough to allow the fibers to be dyed to spread out.
2. Add water, if possible hard water, to obtain a ratio of approximately 1:20 (see Water, p. 26).

   If using soft water, add one teaspoon of chalk per 2.5 gallons (10 liters) of water. Check the pH of the bath and, if necessary, add a little washing soda to achieve a pH between 7 and 8.
3. Add the mordanted fibers, (presoaked and wrung out). Make sure they are completely immersed in the dye bath.
4. Turn on the heat and gradually raise the temperature to a simmer (185–195°F/85–90°C). Maintain this temperature for 20 to 60 minutes.

   Stir regularly (approximately every 10 minutes) and gently. Turn off the heat and allow the dye bath to cool.

   For silk, the dye bath can be made cold, or even in lukewarm water, leaving the fibers to soak for 12 hours and stirring regularly.
5. Once the bath has cooled, remove the fibers and wring out to dry. Dry out of direct sunlight. Finally, wash with the usual precautions (see Washing, p. 58). However, if, as in my case, your water has very little calcium and is slightly acidic, washing with a little dish soap or chalk will intensify the yellow.

White wildflowers

Yarrow, chamomile, wild carrot

Achillea millefolium, Matricaria chamomilla, Daucus carota

- **Part of plant:** flowering tops.
- **Harvesting period:** during summer, when in full bloom.
- **Recommended quantity:** at least 400% fresh plant material in relation to the weight of fiber to be dyed (use of fresh plants is recommended).
- **Color range:** palette of more or less bright yellows with greenish or tawny tones.
- **Type of fiber to be dyed and mordant:** suitable for all fibers. For deeper yellows, use tea, knotweed leaf, or even symplocos as a mordant.

- They are there, seemingly out of nowhere, occupying spaces abandoned by humans, like wastelands, dry roadsides, the edges of rural paths, dry meadows, and sunny corners of the garden.
- Wild, charming, and naturally graceful, they always amaze us when they come into the garden: strong-willed, hardy, and able to live on very little, they discreetly make themselves at home alongside the cultivated flowers, adding a touch of poetry that delights me. The reflection of summer evening light on wild carrot flowers is truly enchanting.
- As common wild plants, they are often considered undesirable, but they were once considered useful.
- The ancients used the aerial parts of wild carrots for their diuretic properties. As for yarrow, its therapeutic use is very similar to that of chamomile: both are recognized for their anti-inflammatory and antibacterial properties.
- The shades of yellow offered by these wild beauties will vary according to the time of harvest, the season, the type of mordant plant you choose, and the temperature and duration of simmering. I have found the yellows to be slightly greenish when picked early in the season, at cooking temperatures below 185°F (85°C).
-

RECIPE

First step: decoction

1. Place the finely chopped flowers in a saucepan. Only the chamomile flowers will be left whole. Cover with water to immerse the plant material. Leave overnight.
2. Heat to just below a gentle simmer (185–195°F/85–90°C). If necessary, add washing soda for a pH of 8. Maintain this temperature for 45 to 60 minutes for more acidic yellows. For darker yellows, raise the temperature slightly. Simmering time will depend on the quantity of plant, from 30 to 90 minutes. Add water if evaporation occurs in order to keep the plant material submerged.
3. Turn off the heat. Cool and strain the decoction through a cheesecloth. Allow the dye liquid to mature for a few hours.

Second step: dyeing

1. Pour the dye liquid into a pot large enough to allow the fibers to be dyed to spread out.
2. Add water to obtain a ratio of approximately 1:20 (see Water, p. 26). Check the bath pH. If necessary, add washing soda dissolved in hot water for a pH of 8.
3. Dip the mordanted fibers (presoaked and wrung out) into the bath. Make sure they are completely immersed in the dye bath.
4. Turn on the heat and gradually increase the temperature. Leave just below simmering (175°F/80°C) or at a gentle simmer (185°F/85°C), depending on the desired shade, for 30 to 60 minutes. Be sure to add hot water during cooking to keep the fibers submerged. Stir regularly (approximately every 10 minutes) and gently. Turn off the heat and allow the dye bath to cool.

   For silk, you can make the dye bath cold, leaving the fibers to soak for 12 hours and stirring regularly.
5. Once the bath has cooled, remove the fibers and wring out to dry. Dry out of direct sunlight. Finally, wash with the usual precautions (see Washing, p. 58).

Saint-John's-wort

Hypericum perforatum

- **Part of plant:** flowering tops preferred, but the whole plant is dyeable.
- **Harvesting period:** during summer, at the start of flowering.
- **Recommended quantity:** at least 400% of the weight of fibers to be dyed for fresh plants. 100–150% for dried plants. Saint-John's-wort is richer in dye when dried.
- **Color range:** yellow, tawny, pink, pinkish-brown.
- **Type of fibers to be dyed and mordant:** suitable for all fibers. Saint-John's-wort has a better affinity with animal fibers. For shades of yellow on wool or silk, mordanting should be done with symplocos.

- A perennial of the Hypericaceae family, Saint-John's-wort is a very common plant. In France, where I live, it can be found at altitudes of up to 6,500 feet (2,000 meters). You'll find it on roadsides, road embankments, wastelands, meadows, and even in your own garden. An undemanding plant in terms of soil type, it requires only sun and is not afraid of drought. Its adaptability makes it a pioneer plant.
- It is easily recognized by its small, sunlike flowers with five bright yellow petals and its small, oval leaves that appear to be pierced by a thousand tiny holes. Hence its full name, "perforate Saint-John's-wort."
- Since ancient times, it has been used to treat wounds and burns, thanks to its antiseptic and anti-inflammatory properties.
- In the fifteenth century, the famous Swiss physician Paracelsus identified Saint-John's-wort as a "devil-may-care" plant that could soothe melancholic souls.
- Today, there is no shortage of scientific studies on Saint-John's-wort in the treatment of mild to moderate depression.
- Saint-John's-wort flowers are edible and are a perfect addition to any salad.
- Add a handful of flowers to a bottle three-quarters full of olive oil and leave to macerate in the sun for three weeks, and you will have a perfect massage oil for soothing sunburn or low back pain.
- The diversity of its chemical compounds explains the wide range of colors that can be obtained with Saint-John's-wort, depending on the process used.

RECIPE

First step: decoction

1. Place the finely chopped flowering sprigs in a saucepan. Cover with water to immerse the plant material. Leave to stand overnight.
2. Bring to a gentle simmer (185–195°F/85–90°C). Maintain this temperature for 45 to 60 minutes, depending on the quantity of plant material. Add water if evaporation occurs in order to keep the plant material submerged.
3. Turn off the heat. Cool and strain the decoction through cheesecloth. Leave the dye liquid to stand overnight.

Second step: dyeing

1. Pour the dye liquid into a stockpot large enough to allow the fibers to be dyed to spread out.
2. Add water to obtain a ratio of approximately 1:20 (see Water, p. 26). Check the bath pH. On wool, a pH of around 4 will produce pinkish tones. In this case, add lemon juice. With a pH of 7 on animal fibers mordanted with symplocos, the shades will be yellow.
3. Dip the mordanted fibers (presoaked and wrung out) into the bath. Make sure they are completely immersed.
4. Turn on the heat and gradually raise the temperature to a boiling point (185–195°F/85–90°C). Boil for 30 to 60 minutes, adding hot water to keep the fibers submerged. Stir regularly (approximately every 10 minutes) and gently. Turn off the heat and allow the dye bath to cool.

   For silk, you can make the dye bath cold, leaving the fibers to soak for 12 hours and stirring regularly.
5. Once the bath has cooled, remove the fibers and wring out to dry. Dry out of direct sunlight. Finally, wash with the usual precautions (see Washing, p. 58).

Calluna

Heather

Calluna vulgaris

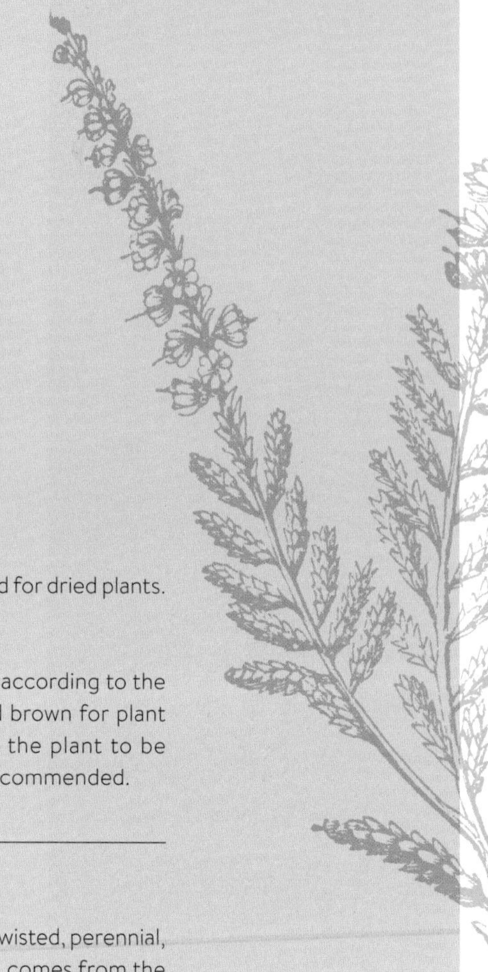

- **Part of plant:** flowering branches.
- **Harvesting period:** late summer, early autumn.
- **Recommended quantity:** 100–200% of the weight of fiber to be dyed for dried plants. 200–400% for fresh plants.
- **Color range:** yellow, orange-yellow, pink, pinkish-brown.
- **Type of fibers to be dyed and mordant:** shades differ considerably according to the nature of the fibers: yellow and orange for animal fibers, pink and brown for plant fibers. Mordanting is necessary. Shades will vary according to the plant to be mordanted and the pH. For yellows on wool or silk, symplocos is recommended.

- Callune heather is not botanically a heather, but actually a callune, a twisted, perennial, evergreen subshrub in the Ericaceae family. Its Latin name, *calluna*, comes from the Greek meaning "to beautify, to make beautiful," a name in memory of the ancient use of heather to make brooms.
- Heather characteristically grows in poor, acidic soils.
- It can be found widely in Europe, in moors, open woods, and at the edges of forests. Very common in France's Massif Central, it colors bare summits a beautiful purplish-pink. Calluna can be confused with the closely related ashy heather, found more in the western half of France.
- It is an extremely hardy plant. Resistant to cold and drought, it has incredible longevity, living up to forty years! It develops an extensive root system that shelters soil fungi. This association enables it to better absorb mineral elements, which are particularly useful in the poor, acidic environments in which it grows.
- Its small, bell-shaped pink flowers attract foraging insects. In herbal medicine, heather is recommended for the prevention and treatment of urinary tract infections.
- At the end of summer, you can pick up a few armfuls of flowering sprigs, observing the rules to avoid harming biodiversity. Calluna can be used fresh or dried.

RECIPE

First step: decoction

1. Place the finely cut flowering sprigs in a saucepan. Cover with water to immerse the plant. Leave to stand overnight.
2. Bring to a low simmer (185–195°F/85–90°C). Maintain this temperature for 45 to 60 minutes, depending on the quantity of plant material. Add water if evaporation occurs in order to keep the plant submerged.
3. Turn off the heat. Cool and strain the decoction through cheesecloth. Reserve the dye liquid.

Second step: dyeing

1. Pour the dye liquid into a stockpot large enough to allow the fibers to be dyed to spread out.
2. Add water to obtain a ratio of approximately 1:20 (see Water, p. 26).

   Check bath pH. On wool, with a pH of around 6, you'll get more orangey-yellow shades. If that is not your desired shade, add a little lemon juice. On the other hand, with a pH of 8 and above, shades will be more pink, especially on plant fibers. In that case, add washing soda dissolved in hot water if that is not your desired shade.
3. Submerge the mordanted fibers (presoaked and wrung out) into the bath. Make sure they are completely immersed.
4. Turn on the heat and gradually raise the temperature to a boil (185–195°F/85–90°C). Boil for 30 to 60 minutes, adding hot water to keep the fibers submerged. Stir regularly (approximately every 10 minutes) and gently. Turn off the heat and allow the dye bath to cool.

   For silk, you can make the dye bath cold, leaving the fibers to soak for 12 hours and stirring regularly.
5. Once the bath has cooled, remove the fibers and wring them out to dry. Dry out of direct sunlight. Finally, wash with the usual precautions (see Washing, p. 58).

Bitter dock

Rumex obtusifolius

- **Part of plant:** seeded stems.
- **Harvesting period:** late summer and autumn.
- **Recommended quantity:** at least 400% dry plant material in relation to the weight of fiber to be dyed.
- **Color range:** orange, salmon, pink, pinkish-brown.
- **Type of fibers to be dyed and mordant:** suitable for all fibers. Shades will be more orange on animal fibers and more pinkish on plant fibers. Mordanting is optional, but strongly recommended.

- *Rumex* is great for making color.
- A perennial herb belonging to the Polygonaceae family, the *Rumex* genus comprises sixty varieties. According to botanist Gérard Ducer, a specialist in soil health bio-indicator plants, almost all of these varieties are indicative of degraded soil: destruction of the clay-humus complex necessary for soil fertility, organic matter, and waterlogging on compacted soils.
- Within the *Rumex* genus, a distinction is made between between docks and sorrels. The former, such as *Rumex alpinus*, *Rumex patienta*, *Rumex obtusifolius*, and *Rumex crispus*, are widespread. They are found throughout Europe and in parts of North America.
- The best-known sorrel is *Rumex acetosa*. It is the sorrel of gardens, and has long been cultivated as a vegetable. It grows wild in slightly acidic meadows. It is the only *Rumex* species that indicates balanced soil. If you have any in your garden, that is a good sign.
- *Rumex* leaves, rich in oxalic acid (the level of which depends on the variety and maturity of the plant), can be used to mordant wool in a pretty yellow (see Plants rich in oxalic acid, p. 37). The long taproots of docks, rich in tannins and iron, can also be used as a mordant plant after being dried and ground.
- But dock can also be a source of color, thanks to the colored tannins and quinones in its aerial parts and in greater quantities in its roots.
- For deeper shades, I recommend mordanting beforehand, either with the leaves if you are dyeing wool or with the roots, if you are dyeing cotton.

RECIPE

First step: decoction

1. Put the crushed stems in a saucepan. Cover with enough water to fully immerse the plant.
2. Bring to a simmer (185–195°F/85–90°C). Maintain this temperature for 45 to 60 minutes, depending on the quantity of plant material. Add water if evaporation occurs in order to keep the plant submerged.
3. Turn off the heat. Cool and strain the decoction through cheesecloth. Reserve the dye liquid.

Second step: dyeing

1. Pour the dye liquid into a stockpot large enough to allow the fibers to be dyed to spread out.
2. Add water to obtain a ratio of approximately 1:20 (see Water, p. 26). Check the bath pH. For pinker shades on plant fibers, add washing soda to achieve a pH of 8.
3. Dip the mordanted fibers (presoaked and wrung out) into the bath. Make sure they are completely immersed.
4. Turn on the heat and gradually raise the temperature to a boil (185–195°F/85–90°C). Boil for about 1 hour, adding hot water to keep the fibers submerged.

   Stir regularly (approximately every 10 minutes) and gently. Turn off the heat and allow the dye bath to cool.

   For silk, you can make the dye bath cold, leaving the fibers to soak for 12 hours and stirring regularly.
5. Once the bath has cooled, remove the fibers and wring out to dry. Dry out of direct sunlight. Finally, wash with the usual precautions (see Washing, p. 58).

IN THE SHADE OF FORESTS AND HEDGES: TREES AND SHRUBS

What would we do without trees? Their "contemplation fills my heart with love," wrote Victor Hugo in his magnificent poem "To the Trees." A sentiment that, alas, seems not to have been shared by all.

The evocation of trees today leaves little room for poetry. It has been replaced by a cry of alarm from scientists about the urgent need to combat deforestation and preserve trees and hedges in an attempt to mitigate the effects of climate change and protect ecosystems.

So I can only encourage you to plant trees wherever you can. By choosing species with tinctorial properties—and there are many of them—you will be helping to maintain the biodiversity that is so essential to us all.

Tree leaves

Birch, walnut

Betula pendula, Juglans regia

- **Part of plant:** leaves.
- **Harvesting period:** spring to late summer.
- **Recommended quantity:** at least 400% of the weight of the fiber to be dyed for fresh plant materials. 100–200% for dried plant materials.
- **Color range:** shades of yellow.
- **Type of fibers to be dyed and mordant:** for bright yellows, best suited to animal fibers mordanted with symplocos.

- Tree leaves are a very accessible source of color. Easy to pick in large quantities, leaves are easy to dry and crush.
- Most tree leaves are rich in flavonoids. Concentrations of colorants vary from species to species. Likewise, as the chemical composition of leaves changes over the seasons, the shades will differ depending on whether you pick them in spring or late summer. It is up to you to experiment with the trees around you: pistachio trees, lime trees, elder trees, and ash trees. Fig tree leaves picked early in the season can make a lovely soft green.
- Here's a hint to help you identify flavonoid-rich leaves: observe their colors in autumn. Leaves that have turned orange-yellow indicate the presence of flavonoids, which become visible as the chlorophyll gradually disappears under the effect of lower levels of sunlight.
- Note that some leaves are also rich in tannins of varying hues, which can darken the shades produced. For example, I obtained a lovely amber-brown color from the leaves of the Judas tree.
- The walnut tree, from its leaf to its bark to its fruit, is a veritable "factory" of colorants: its bark and fruit will give you solid browns without any prior mordanting, thanks to the combination of tannins and juglone. As for the leaves, they contain flavonoids such as quercetin, which are responsible for the yellow color.
- Birch, which I have already mentioned, is a kind of multipurpose plant for dyeing. A wool mordant plant (see p. 39), it is also a substantive color plant (see Glossary, p. 175). The leaves, for their part, produce very luminous yellows on wool.

RECIPE

First step: decoction

1. Put the finely chopped leaves in a saucepan. Cover with water and leave overnight.
2. Turn on the heat, gradually increasing the temperature to a simmer (185–195°F/85–90°C). Maintain this temperature for 20 to 60 minutes, depending on the quantity of plant material.
3. Turn off the heat. Cool and strain the decoction through cheesecloth. Reserve the dye liquid.

Second step: dyeing

1. Pour the dye liquid into a stockpot large enough to allow the fibers to be dyed to spread out.
2. Add water to obtain a ratio of approximately 1:20 (see Water, p. 26). Check the pH of the bath and add a little washing soda if necessary to achieve a pH of 7 to 8.
3. Add the fibers (presoaked and wrung out), mordanted if necessary. Make sure they are completely immersed in the bath.
4. Turn on the heat and gradually raise the temperature to a simmer (185–195°F/85–90°C). Maintain this temperature for 20 to 60 minutes.

   Stir regularly (approximately every 10 minutes) and gently. Turn off the heat and allow the dye bath to cool.

   For silk, the dye bath can be made cold, or even in lukewarm water, leaving the fibers to soak for 12 hours and stirring regularly.
5. Once the bath has cooled, remove the fibers and wring out to dry. Dry out of direct sunlight. Finally, wash with the usual precautions (see Washing, p. 58).

Birch

The tree of wisdom

Betula pendula

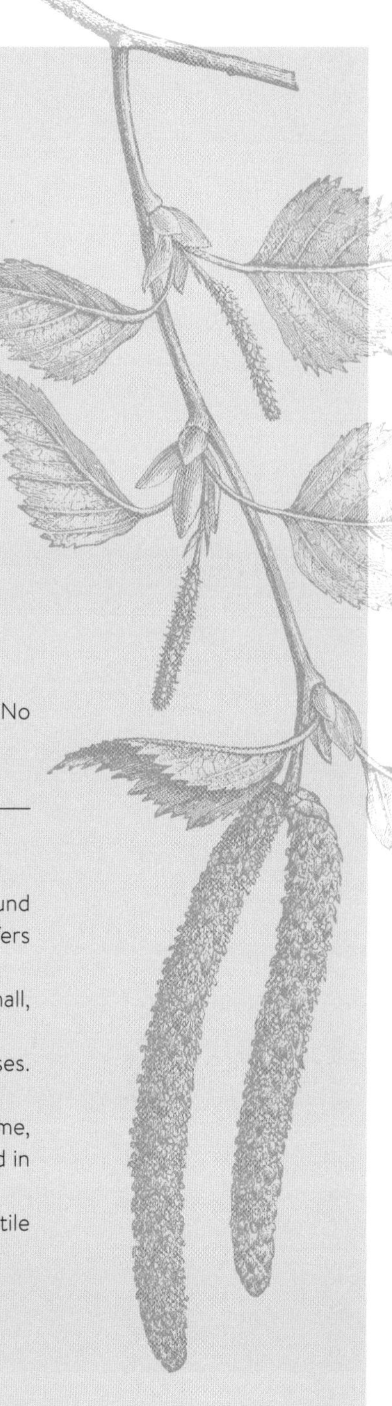

- **Part of plant:** bark.
- **Harvesting period:** year-round.
- **Recommended quantity:** at least 100% of the weight of fiber to be dyed.
- **Color range:** shades of pink.
- **Type of fibers to be dyed and mordant:** suitable for both animal and plant fibers. No mordanting required.

- Birch, a member of the Betulaceae family, is a tree that grows spontaneously around my home. It is a pioneer species that colonizes the wasteland left behind after conifers have been cut down. Birch thrives in cool, acidic soils and is a fast-growing tree.
- It is easily recognized by its white bark, which appears on older trees, and its small, serrated leaves.
- Birch trees are found throughout Europe and North America. They have many uses. In carpentry, their wood is used to make tools, objects, and furniture.
- However, it is the medicinal properties of birch that have made it a household name, with the famous birch water. Rich in trace elements and polyphenols, harvested in spring, it is generally consumed to help detoxify the body.
- The bark, for its part, has a high content of colorful tannins, which can give textile fibers a lovely pinkish hue.

RECIPE

First step: decoction

1. Place the crushed or powdered bark in a saucepan. Cover with water to immerse the plant. Leave to stand overnight.
2. Bring to a simmer (185–195°F/85–90°C). During cooking, add baking soda to bring the pH to 8. The liquid will turn pink. Maintain this temperature for 45 to 90 minutes, depending on the quantity of plant material. Add water if evaporation occurs in order to keep the plant submerged.
3. Turn off the heat. Cool and strain the decoction through cheesecloth. Reserve the dye liquid.

   For a higher concentration of colorant, you can repeat these steps and make a second decoction with the plant material recovered from the cheesecloth. Add the second dye liquid to the first.

   Leave the resulting dye liquid to stand overnight.

Second step: dyeing

1. Pour the dye liquid into a stockpot large enough to allow the fibers to be dyed to spread out.
2. Add enough water to obtain a ratio of approximately 1:20 (see Water, p. 26). Check the bath pH, which should be between 7 and 8. Add washing soda if necessary.
3. Add the fibers (presoaked and wrung out). Make sure they are completely immersed in the bath.
4. Turn on the heat and gradually increase the temperature to a boil (185–195°F/85–90°C). Boil for 30 to 60 minutes, adding hot water as needed to keep the fibers submerged. Stir regularly (approximately every 10 minutes) and gently. Turn off the heat and allow the dye bath to cool.

   For silk, you can make the dye bath cold, leaving the fibers to soak for 12 hours and stirring regularly.
5. Once the bath has cooled, remove the fibers and wring out to dry. Dry out of direct sunlight. Finally, wash with the usual precautions (see Washing, p. 58).

Alder buckthorn

Frangula alnus

- **Part of plant:** bark.
- **Harvesting period:** spring.
- **Recommended quantity:** at least 100% of the weight of fiber to be dyed.
- **Color range:** shades of golden yellow.
- **Type of fibers to be dyed and mordant:** best suited to animal fibers with any type of mordant.

- Belonging to the Rhamnaceae family, alder buckthorn is a spontaneous shrub found in damp undergrowth, clearings, and marshy areas. It prefers heavy, calcareous soils. It is found throughout Europe, with the exception of the Mediterranean basin. In North America, it can be found in the northeast. Its charming, little white flowers that appear in the spring are a great source of honey. And its fruits—small, green berries that turn black when ripe—are much appreciated by birds.
- Buckthorn is well-known to dyers. In his book of experiments making plant-based dyes on wool, Louis-Alexandre Dambourney (see p. 39) successfully experimented with making dye from its berries, both green and ripe. Having obtained bright yellows with the former, he was very pleased with the blue-violet color obtained with the latter.
- As alder buckthorn doesn't grow wild near my home, I haven't been able to experiment with it. I have, however, been able to make dye from the bark. Known in herbal medicine for its laxative effect, it can easily be purchased from an herbalist.
- If alder buckthorn grows near you, you can harvest the bark from young trunks and twigs in March and April. It can be used fresh or dried. Dried bark, however, produces brighter shades.
- Rich in yellow and reddish colorants, the bark can be used to make beautiful golden yellows.
- Other kinds of buckthorn shrubs from the *Rhamnus* genus, often confused with alder buckthorn, can offer similar hues.

RECIPE

First step: decoction

1 Place the or powdered bark in a saucepan. Cover with enough water to fully immerse the plant. Leave to stand overnight.
2 Turn on the heat and bring to a simmer (185–195°F/85–90°C). During cooking, add lemon juice to obtain a pH of 4. Maintain this temperature for 30 to 60 minutes, depending on the quantity of plant material. Add water if evaporation occurs in order to keep the plant submerged.
3 Turn off the heat. Cool and strain the decoction through cheesecloth. Reserve the dye liquid.

For a higher concentration of colorant, you can repeat these steps and make a second decoction with the plant material recovered through the cheesecloth. Add the second dye liquid to the first.

Second step: dyeing

1 Pour the dye liquid into a stockpot large enough to allow the fibers to be dyed to spread out.
2 Add water to obtain a ratio of approximately 1:20 (see Water, p. 26). Check the pH of the bath, which should be around 4 or 5. Add lemon juice if necessary.
3 Add the mordanted fibers (presoaked and wrung out). Make sure they are completely immersed in the bath.
4 Turn on the heat and gradually raise the temperature to a boil (185–195°F/85–90°C). Boil for 30 to 60 minutes, adding hot water as needed to keep the fibers submerged. Stir regularly (approximately every 10 minutes) and gently. Turn off the heat and allow the dye bath to cool.

For silk, you can make the dye bath cold, leaving the fibers to soak for 12 hours and stirring regularly.

5 Once the bath has cooled, remove the fibers and wring out to dry. Dry away from direct sunlight. Finally, wash with the usual precautions (see Washing, p. 58).

Harlequin glorybower

Clerodendrum trichotomum

- **Part of plant:** fresh berries.
- **Harvesting period:** late summer, early autumn.
- **Recommended quantity:** 100% of the weight of fiber to be dyed, or even more for a deeper color.
- **Color range:** blue.
- **Type of fibers to be dyed and mordant:** can be used to dye both animal and plant fibers. Works very well with silk. No mordant required.

- The harlequin glorybower, also known as the "lucky tree," is a shrub native to East Asia. It is widespread in China, Japan, and India, where it is considered a medicinal plant. Its leaves are used for their anti-inflammatory and antihistaminic properties. Once considered a sacred plant, it was used by Ceylonese priests during their ceremonies.
- Introduced to Europe in the nineteenth century by Mr. Siebold, a physician and naturalist, it is now planted in gardens and parks as an ornamental plant. Its light shade, sweet jasmine-like fragrance, and delicate pinkish flowers, which attract all kinds of pollinating insects, make it a shrub of incomparable romantic charm. And in late summer, it surprises us with small turquoise-blue berries forming in the center of a crimson-pink calyx. But the blue pearls are not only decorative.
- According to Japanese studies, ripe berries contain trichotomine, a dye belonging to the indigoid family, which, unlike indigo, is water-soluble when the fruit is fresh. So obviously, for the dyer, this shrub is of particular interest.
- A few years ago, I planted a *Clerodendrum* plant in my garden. It likes a sheltered position in sun or half shade, in rich, cool, draining soil. It grows relatively quickly and produces suckers easily. Once well established, it is therefore easy to propagate in the garden.
- When the flowering ends and berries appear, I keep an eye on them: the birds love these fruits. So it is important to choose the right moment to pick as many ripe berries as possible and make dye with them immediately. To preserve their freshness, which is essential for dyeing, you can freeze them.

RECIPE

First step: decoction

1 Put the berries in a saucepan and cover with water.
2 Gradually increase the temperature to a simmer (185–195°F/85–90°C). During cooking, crush the berries with a fork or potato masher to release as much colorant as possible.
3 Simmer for 5 to 20 minutes, depending on the quantity of plant material. The liquid will turn blue and the berry shells will discolor.
4 Turn off the heat. Cool and strain the decoction through cheesecloth. Reserve the dye liquid.

Second step: dyeing

1 Pour the dye liquid into a stockpot large enough to allow the fibers to be dyed to spread out.
2 Add water to obtain a ratio of approximately 1:20 (see Water, p. 26).
3 Add the fibers (presoaked and wrung out). Make sure they are completely immersed in the dye bath.
4 Heat and gradually raise the temperature to 175°F (80°C), and maintain for at least 20 minutes.

   Stir regularly (approximately every 10 minutes) and gently.
5 Dyeing can be considered complete when the dye liquid has lost its blue color and the dye has been completely absorbed by the fibers. Turn off the heat and allow the dye bath to cool.

   For silk, the dye bath can be made in cold or even lukewarm water, leaving the fibers to soak for 12 hours and stirring regularly.
6 Once the bath has cooled, take out the fibers, which will have a more or less intense sky-blue color. Wring them out and dry them away from direct sunlight. Finally, wash with the usual precautions (see Washing, p. 58).

Black elderberry

Sambucus nigra

- **Part of plant:** fresh, dark berries.
- **Harvesting period:** late summer.
- **Recommended quantity:** 400% of the weight of fiber to be dyed.
- **Color range:** purplish-pink, blue.
- **Type of fibers to be dyed and mordant:** suitable for all fibers, animal and plant, with any type of mordant. A beet leaf mordant is recommended for animal fibers.

- A large shrub in the Adoxaceae family, black elderberry is widespread in rural areas. A spontaneous plant around hedges and the edges of forests, it likes to settle where it is least expected. The ruins of old stone houses are a habitat it particularly appreciates.
- Black elderberry should be distinguished from Danewort (*Sambucus ebulus*), whose berries are poisonous. Unlike black elderberry, it is a smaller herbaceous plant, with no wood or trunk.
- It is easy to invite black elderberry into your garden. Propagation by cuttings from young twigs in autumn or early summer works very well.
- In the garden, it plays host to aphids and blackbirds. The strong smell of its leaves scares off field mice. Leaf slurry can be useful in the fight against rose blight.
- In the past, it was customary to plant a black elderberry near the house. It had the reputation of being "the rural pharmacy." All parts of the plant have medicinal properties. The berries, rich in antioxidants, have anti-inflammatory properties thanks to their high anthocyanin content.
- It is precisely these anthocyanins that interest us for dyeing. Elderberries have been used for their color for centuries. In the eighteenth century, they were used to dye wool mordanted with alum to a musk color, reputed to be long-lasting. As its berries are also rich in tannins, lavender blues can be obtained from linen treated with iron water.
- Anthocyanins are very sensitive to variations in pH (see p. 22), so it is not easy to preserve the purplish-pink color of berry juice on textile fibers. However, in my experiments, wool mordanted with beet leaves in solar dyeing gave satisfactory results in terms of color stability.

RECIPE

First step: extract production

1. Put the berries in an airtight bucket or jar. Cover with rainwater and add white vinegar to obtain a pH of around 4 to 5.
2. Close the jar and place it in the sun, on or against a stone wall. If summer temperatures are very high, check the temperature of the maceration, which should not exceed 140°F (60°C).
3. Forget about the jar for a little while, at least 2 or 3 days, up to a month; there's no real rule here. It all depends on the weather. Check the color of your bath: you can consider the process complete once it has taken on a nice red color.
4. Strain the liquid using a strainer and a cheesecloth. For a stronger concentration, crush the berries left in the cheesecloth with a pestle, potato masher, or other device, and add this dye liquid to the first. Reserve the dye liquid.

Second step: dyeing

1. Pour the dye liquid into a sealable bucket or jar large enough to allow the fibers to be dyed to spread out.
2. Add the beet-leaf-mordanted fibers (presoaked and wrung out). Add rainwater if necessary, so that the fibers are completely submerged. Close the container.
3. Leave the container in the sun. Check the temperature regularly, which should not exceed 140°F (60°C) and stir every 2 to 3 days to ensure an even tone. You can consider the dyeing process complete once you have achieved your desired shade.
4. Take out the fibers, wring them out and dry them out of direct sunlight. Finally, wash them in fresh water with a little lemon juice to preserve the pink's radiance.

GLOSSARY

Colorant A colorant is water-soluble. Most dye plants contain colorants, which are generally extracted by decoction.

Colorfast A color is said to be colorfast when it is resistant to light, UV rays, washing, rubbing, and pH variations. Laboratories test dyes for colorfastness. Results are generally classified on a scale of 1 to 8.

Decoction The act of simmering plants immersed in water.

Fermentation The act of leaving plants in generally acidic water for prolonged periods in a hermetically sealed container and allowing bacteria to "digest" the plant matter.

Galling The process of treating a fabric with a tannin bath, generally a gallnut bath.

Inputs Term used in agriculture to designate the various products added to crops, such as fertilizers, pesticides, and all plant protection products in general.

Level Term used to designate a homogeneous color throughout the textile fiber.

Maceration The act of soaking plants in cold or warm water.

Mordanting The process of soaking a textile fiber in a mordant, which enables the dye to adhere to the fiber so that the color holds.

Mulesing An Australian technique that involves cutting away excess skin from the hindquarters of lambs to prevent parasitic infection. Numerous animal protection associations are fighting against this practice, which is considered cruel. The Responsible Wool Standard (RWS) label guarantees mulesing-free wool.

pH Stands for "potential of hydrogen." It is used to measure the acidic or basic character of a solution, such as a decoction or a dye bath. The higher the number (above 7), the more basic the solution. Conversely, the lower the number (below 7), the more acidic the solution.

Pigment A pigment is insoluble in water. Indigo plants contain a pigment. The indigo vat process solubilizes the indigo pigment.

Pioneer plant A plant capable of colonizing an area devoid of vegetation. Its development allows the soil to be "worked" to make way for more diversified vegetation.

Simmer The act of bringing a liquid to a low boil at 185–195°F (85–90°C).

Substantive (color) Term used for dyeing plants whose dyeing agents adhere directly to the fiber to be dyed, without the need for a mordant. It contrasts with "adjective" color, a dye plant that requires mordanting to produce color.

Superwash (wool) Wool that has undergone chemical treatment to prevent felting in the wash.

Tannin A chemical compound found widely in the plant world, which binds to proteins and metals. A distinction is made between hydrolyzable tannins, which are generally lightly colored and include gallotannins and ellagitannins, and condensed tannins, also known as proanthocyanidins. The latter produce reddish-brown hues.

ACKNOWLEDGMENTS

To Magali Bontoux and Michel Garcia for their generosity and professionalism. I learned a lot from them and was able to find my way.

To Anne Serroy, who convinced me to dare to write this book and who accompanied me throughout this wonderful adventure.

To Marie Baumann, for all her confidence. She believed in my work, both as an artisan in plant color and as a photographer. Without her, this book would not have been possible.

To the whole Hoëbeke team, Louise, and Fanny, for the stimulating and enriching teamwork.

To Aliénor, for her knowledge of lacto-fermented juice, which enabled me to experiment with beet color.

To Laura from Fleurs du Brionnais, Coraline and Romain from Terre Nouvelle, and Ferme des Herbes Folles, who kindly opened the doors of their farms so that I could glean a few plants here and there.

To all those who have faithfully followed my work over the years. Their support and many testimonials have given me the confidence to continue along this path I have decided to follow. Without them, the idea for this book would never have taken root.

To Jeanne, Charles, and Jean, the colors of my life.

To Pearly, my dog, my harvesting companion.

First published in the United States of America in 2025 by
Rizzoli International Publications, Inc.
49 West 27th Street
New York, NY 10001
www.rizzoliusa.com

Originally published in French in 2023 as
Teinture sauvage : De la plante à la couleur. Initiation à la teinture végétale by
Gallimard, collection Hoëbeke, Paris, France
www.gallimard.fr

For Rizzoli
Publisher: Charles Miers
Editor: Klaus Kirschbaum
Assistant Editor: Emily Ligniti
Managing Editor: Lynn Scrabis
Translator: Christiana Hills

ISBN: 978-0-8478-4546-0
Library of Congress Control Number: 2024945016

Printed in Slovenia
2025 2026 2027 2028 / 10 9 8 7 6 5 4 3 2 1

Visit us online:
Instagram.com/RizzoliBooks
Facebook.com/RizzoliNewYork
X: @Rizzoli_Books
Youtube.com/user/RizzoliNY